The Stars of Earth

# THE STARS OF EARTH

NEW AND SELECTED POEMS

BY
Emily Grosholz

WORLD GALAXY PRESS
An imprint of Able Muse Press

Copyright ©2017 by Emily Grosholz
First published in 2017 by

# Word Galaxy Press

www.wordgalaxy.com

All rights reserved. No part of this book may be used or reproduced in any manner whatsoever without written permission except in the case of brief quotations embedded in critical articles and reviews. Requests for permission should be e-mailed to editor@ablemuse.com for the attention of the Word Galaxy Press editor.

Printed in the United States of America

Library of Congress Control Number: 2017930375

ISBN 978-1-77349-001-4 (paperback)
ISBN 978-1-77349-005-2 (hardcover)
ISBN 978-1-77349-000-7 (digital)

Cover and interior book drawings by Farhad Ostovani

Cover & book design by Alexander Pepple

Word Galaxy Press is an imprint of Able Muse Press—at
www.ablemusepress.com

Word Galaxy Press
467 Saratoga Avenue #602
San Jose, CA 95129

*This book is dedicated to the memory of*

*Yves Bonnefoy, Maxin Kumin, Frederick Morgan, and Donald Davie*

*Contents*

A Year (2016)

5   October
- Love's Shadow   *5*
- Ode to the Butterflies   *6*
- First Piano Lesson   *7*
- Among Cosmologists   *8*
- The Always Coming On   *9*
- Where the Wild Things Are   *10*

11   November
- November   *11*
- In Praise of Fractals   *12*
- The Choir   *15*
- Canvassing for Mr. Obama   *16*
- What a Poet Wants   *17*

18   December
- Twelfth Night   *18*
- Technical Divination   *19*
- The House of Trees   *22*
- Justice   *23*
- Holding Pattern   *26*

27   January
- Not Summer   *27*
- The Warning   *28*
- Days of 1983   *29*

  On Painting *31*
  The Kitchen Window *34*

*35* February
  No Moon *35*
  Forsythia *36*
  Morning Delivery of *The Times* *37*
  While You Lay Sleeping *39*
  *Ut musica pictura* *40*
  Snowdrop *41*
  Elegy *42*
  Counterpane *44*

*45* March
  Spring Cleaning *45*
  Two Meditations on Stone *46*
  What I Forgot, What I Could Not Forget *48*
  Leaving the Garden *49*
  Goodbye to State College *50*

*51* April
  April 7, 2011 *51*
  On Pilgrim Hill *52*
  The Beautiful Game *54*
  Mind *56*
  Leaves and Clouds *57*
  Where I Went, and Cannot Come Again *58*

*59* May
  Not Roses *59*
  Uncertain *60*
  Insomnia *61*
  Two Passages from Colette *62*
  Just a Star *64*

*65* June
  Silver *65*
  The Art of Glassblowing *66*

      Elliptic Curves and Modular Forms Converge South of the Taklamakan  *67*

      Primary School  *68*

      The Stars of Earth  *69*

*70*  July

      Here and There  *70*

      Sunset  *71*

      Citizens  *72*

      Astronomy  *73*

      Kisses  *74*

      Equal and Opposite  *75*

*76*  August

      Daylilies  *76*

      Letter from Châtel-Montagne  *77*

      Abbey Road  *78*

      The Tallinn Ferry  *79*

      European Paper  *80*

      Yesterday  *81*

*82*  September

      But They Come Back Again  *82*

      Four from the Berggarten, Hannover  *83*

      Elegy for the Tussey Ridge: Fracking Comes to Central Pennsylvania  *86*

      Bittersweet  *87*

      The Dream of Chaucer  *88*

      Roses  *90*

## The River Painter (1984)

*95*  Gathering of Friends, after the Fall of the Sung Dynasty

*97*  On an Album Leaf by Ma Yuan

*98*  The River Painter

*101*  Belleville, Paris, France

Dinner in the Courtyard  *101*
97 rue Compans  *101*
Souvenir  *103*
In the Garden  *104*
The Last of the Courtyard  *105*

*106*  Greece
On the Ferry, toward Patras  *106*
Galerie Orphée  *107*
In Medias Res  *108*

*109*  Covering Ground: Bicycling, Running, Hiking
Ruins at Jumièges  *109*
Marathon  *110*
Spring Fever  *111*
Edgewood Park  *112*
Following the Dordogne  *113*
Remembering the Ardèche  *115*
Ithaka I  *115*

*117*  Science
The Dissolution of the Rainbow  *117*
Goethe in Verona  *118*
Birds, Trees and Lovers  *120*

*122*  Germany
The Poet and the Canal  *122*
To Cathy Iino  *124*
Letters from a Gardener  *126*
Letter from Germany  *131*
On the Loss of My Mother's Jewelry  *132*

*134*  Mortality
Allhallows  *134*
In the Light of October  *136*
Rodin to Rilke  *137*
The Return  *138*

# Shores and Headlands (1988)

143  The Gold Earrings
145  The End of Summer
147  Nietzsche in the Box of Straws
151  Exchanges
154  Vagabondage in Sonnets
      Saint-Germain, Paris, France   *154*
      Raschplatzhochstraße, Hannover, Germany   *154*
      Mediterranean   *155*
      On the Untersberg, Salzburg, Austria   *156*
      Siesta   *156*
      The Old Fisherman   *157*
158  Letters from La Plata
      Letter from La Plata I   *158*
      Interval   *159*
      Letter from La Plata II   *160*
      Exile   *161*
      Letter from La Plata III   *162*
      Theories of Vision   *163*
      Letter from La Plata IV   *166*
      The Carnival of Dreams   *167*
      Two Variations on a Theme   *168*
171  Roman Elegies
      Side-lit   *171*
      In the Abruzzi   *172*
      The World as Will, Idea, *Grappa,* and Pigeons   *173*
      Another Song   *174*
175  Philosophy
      After *Timaeus*   *175*
      Perceptual Acquaintance   *175*
      Letter from Durham   *176*

*180* Prothalamia
>  The Outer Banks  *180*
>  Open Secrets  *182*
>  The Ratio of Green  *183*
>  The Courtyard Revisited  *185*
>  The Tempest  *186*
>  The Cliffs at Praiano  *188*

# Eden (1992)

*193* On Spadina Avenue
*195* West Wind
*196* Commuter Marriage
*201* Waiting for News of Jackie's Firstborn
*202* Elegy
*203* Pilgrims
*205* Revisiting Philadelphia
>  Dark Tents and Fires  *205*
>  Boundaries  *207*
>  Sidonie  *209*
>  Secret Places of Forrest Lane  *210*
>  The Neolithic Revolution of 1956  *211*
>  Legacies  *213*
>  A Poem for Polly  *214*
>  Life of a Salesman  *217*

*219* Revisiting Paris
>  Symmetry  *219*
>  72 rue Lepic  *221*
>  Belleville Revisited  *222*

*223* A Son
>  Listening  *223*
>  Thirty-Six Weeks  *224*

      Autumn Sonata  *226*

      Romance  *227*

*229*  Cassis

      The Outdoor Market at Cassis  *229*

      Excursion to the Third *Calanque*  *229*

      Rain or Shine  *231*

*233*  Home

      The Pot of Basil  *233*

      Eden  *235*

      The Shape of Desire  *237*

      Proportions of the Heart  *238*

## The Abacus of Years (2002)

*243*  The Abacus of Years

*245*  Anna

*247*  Rondo, Andante

*249*  Ben

      Where the Sky Used to Be  *249*

      Through the Darkness Be Thou Near Me  *250*

      Real Bullets  *251*

      The Great Blizzard  *253*

      Revisiting the Church of the Holy Sepulcher  *255*

*256*  Robbie

      Accident and Essence  *256*

      Adopting Robbie  *257*

      Robbie Discovers Rain  *259*

      Robbie Discovers Puddles  *259*

      Saying Farewell by the Bridge over the Snow River  *261*

      Robbie and I Discover Painting  *262*

      Tour of the Flower Depot at Sanary-sur-Mer  *263*

      Letting the Children Fly  *264*

265 William and Mary-Frances
- Putting on the Ritz  *265*
- Finitude  *266*
- Pirates of the Caribbean  *267*
- How Things Change  *269*
- Fixtures of Smoke  *270*

*271* England
- After the Revolution  *271*
- Trying to Describe the Reals in Cambridge  *272*
- The Freestone Wall and the Walled Garden  *273*
- What Rembrandt Saw  *275*
- Willows  *277*
- A Bouquet for Buffalo  *277*
- Coming Home from England  *279*

*280* More Philosophy
- In Praise of the Humanities  *280*
- Brancusi's Fish as a Figure of Thought  *282*
- Rationalism  *283*
- Café on the rue Gay-Lussac  *284*
- Days of 1984  *285*
- Weathering  *285*
- Rivers  *286*
- The Historian's Pursuit  *290*
- Signing the Darkness  *291*
- Ithaka II  *292*
- Watering  *293*

*295* Acknowledgments

The Stars of Earth

A Year (2016)

# October

### Love's Shadow

Lately the subject of my thought is time:
How time flows like a river, if it does,
Or like a house of crystal, stands immobile,
Or ceases where the very smallest creatures
Dance without houses, clocks, or bankless streams.

Here is my birthday, carried round again
By the tall star-crossed cycles of the moon.
Love's shadow brightens as the day begins
And then grows longer, whether we believe
That time is real or just a dream of things.

## Ode to the Butterflies

Spinoza says you're pure theology: O crazy butterflies aloft
Drinking the last of autumn's flower-wine, as if you thought
There's no tomorrow, as if chicory, vetch and daisies
Weren't on their long last legs, as if the field and forest
Mammals weren't headed underground, as if the coldest
Spells won't cast themselves on us before October's over.
But party, party, party! Spinoza says you're somehow
Cutouts of God's great fabric—matter—divine confetti

Thrown necessarily up in just these handfuls that I see
Right here, right now, and so am I, this slower body
Earthbound as you distractingly, disarmingly, are not.
Mode of the same sweet attribute, just one amidst an infinite,
Uncountable swarm. So we are all eternal, little buddies!
Succession is illusion, look: the sheer cloud-shadow stipple,
Breezes that shake the goldenrod, your upward-gusting trios,
We're all in this together and like God we're always here!

# First Piano Lesson

*For Leslie Beers*

For years they have been pressing the white keys,
Sometimes the black, occasionally, haphazardly
Great fingerfuls together. But where
Exactly was the music, they wondered? Gone.

Today they built a bridge from C to G
As if across Giverny's garden pond.
Perhaps it is a rainbow? G to C,
Aural, slant-visible, inevitable, clear.

They stand amazed around the grand piano
Capable at last of lifting up
From sound's long restlessness the dripping
Glittery net of intervals and in its knotted strings

That golden fish, a song!

# Among Cosmologists

*For Sarah Shandera*

Breathlessly, with a shrug and a vague gesture,
Empty hand palm up, collecting something
From empty space that is by all accounts
Not empty, rather like the four-dimensional
Surface of an $n$-dimensional cauldron
Where bubbles form and wink out of existence,
The young expert on galaxies suggests,
"A hundred billion?" However the next Sloan
Survey announces the count of galaxies—
Red-shifting as they leave us past the tall
Implacable vast light cone we cannot see
But know it marks the boundaries of seeing.

"Doesn't it keep you up at night, this outward
Rush of galaxies fleeing themselves and us
Into the infinite arms of the multiverse?"
I ask. "Oh, no," she answers, catching her breath.
"What keeps me up is our recurrent failure
To know the universe before inflation,
Or offer quantum mechanics a foundation.
It's not the future, but the hidden past.
It's not what's overhead, but underneath."

## The Always Coming On

The sun is closing in on the horizon,
Light pocks the highway like a rain of gold,
And I rush through at seventy, seventy-five.
My husband sees me squint and asks, perhaps,
His baseball cap might help? But I persist
In blocking out the lightfall with my fist,
When suddenly the road shifts north northwest,
The hills get higher and the sun eclipses.
Those lines return: *how swift, how secretly*
*The shadow of the night comes on.* MacLeish.

He sailed to Persia in the nineteen-twenties,
A diplomat who hoped to help dismantle
The opium trade, but fruitlessly. He left
Bewitched, recalling afterward the spell
Onset of evening cast across the desert,
Great vistas of time and space, of dynasties,
So swiftly, silently engulfed, and then
Only the nomads with their tents and fires.

I have to turn the headlights on.
The hills' deep emerald fades to blue,
The sky's cerulean edge to mauve;
My hair falls sideways past my nape,
White as a ghost, and just as thin.
I have to turn the headlights on
To see how far the highway goes,
To pierce the darkness, secret, swift,
The wayward evening, losing light
And warmth, direction, solace, home.

## Where the Wild Things Are

The fields around my country house are sown
With soy and corn. Though corn is fringed and bearded,
Sways with the wind and shudders, speaking in tongues,
Its husks and stalks a sheer archaic murmur, lost
To living memory but able to haunt us still,
And soy is low and green and generally silent,
They're the main crops that cash out for our farmers.
So we can't blame the farmers; they have to live.

And here and there a browsing cow or two
Munches through yellowing hayfields, which distracts
The eye with color and barnstorms the nose.
Yet all in all the crops are sad, and boring:
They won't feed hungry children or restless piglets,
Only the international lust for energy in any
Form, at any cost, a kind of chlorophyllic burn.
That's why, when I go walking across the valley,

I've learned to stick to weedy border farm roads,
Hard to pursue, reverting to vetch or bramble:
Those roads where wilderness asserts itself
In miniature, where clouded sulphurs cluster
Near puddles, and those butterflies we like to call
Coppers, purples, blues, bits of the visible spectrum
Lighter than air, go tumbling over the clover,
And mingle with satyrs, nymphs, and painted ladies!

# November

## November

*For Dick Davis*

My friend, it seems as if we know at last
We won't be here much longer.
Crossing the mountain of a hundred years
We've gained the shadow side. Against our faces
Boreas falls, the breath of nothingness.

The Chinese sages recommend reflection:
Characters like willows
Bend to the river where cold water flows
Unceasingly, changing its fluid mind
With every passing cloud or boat or leaf.

What's left behind? Only a few brief verses.
Come to visit soon, and drink a glass
Of wine and watch the woods behind my house
Decant the autumn moon
Overblown and gold on the horizon.

## In Praise of Fractals

*For Roald Hoffmann and Joseph Mazur*

*Variations on the Introduction to* The Fractal Geometry of Nature *by Benoit Mandelbrot (New York: W. H. Freeman and Company, 1983)*

Euclid's geometry cannot describe,
Nor Apollonius', the shape of mountains,
Puddles, clouds, peninsulas, or trees.
Clouds are never spheres,
Nor mountains cones, nor Ponderosa pines;
Bark is not smooth; and where the land and sea
So variously lie
And lightly kiss, is no hyperbola.

Compared with Euclid's elementary forms,
Nature, loosening her hair, exhibits patterns
(Sweetly disarrayed, afloat, uncombed)
Not simply of a higher degree $n$
But rather of an altogether different
Level of complexity:
The number of her scales of distances
Is almost infinite.

How shall we study the morphology
Of the amorphous? Benoit Mandelbrot
Solved the conundrum by inventing fractals,
A lineage of shapes
Fretted by chance, whose regularities
Are all statistical, like Brownian motion,
Whose fine configurations
Turn out to be the same at every scale.

Some fractal sets are curves
(Space-filling curves!) or complex surfaces;
Others are wholly disconnected "dusts";
Others are just too odd to have a name.
Poincaré once observed,
There may be questions that we choose to ask,
But others ask themselves,
Sometimes for centuries, while no one listens.

Questions that ask themselves without repose
May come to rest at last in someone's mind.
So Mandelbrot in time
Designed his fractal brood to be admired
Not merely for its formal elegance
As mathematical structure,
But power to interpret, curl by curl,
Nature's coiffure of molecules and mountains.

What gentle revolution of ideas
Disjoins the eighteenth century from ours!
Cantor's set of nested missing thirds,
Peano's curve of fractional dimension,
Mandelbrot's fractals, counter the old rule
Of continuity,
Domesticating what shortsightedly
Was once considered monstrous.

Nature embraces monsters as her own,
Encouraging the pensive mathematician
To find anomaly
Inherent in the creatures all around us.
The masters of infinity,
Cantor, Peano, Hausdorff, Mandelbrot,
Discovered sets not in the end transcendent
But immanent, Spinoza's darling Cause.

Imagination shoots the breeze with nature
And what they speak (mathematics) as they flirt
Reveals itself surprisingly effective
In science, a wrought gift
We don't deserve or seek or understand.
So let us just be grateful,
And hope that it goes on, although our joy
Is always balanced by our bafflement.

# The Choir

*For Sara Amadori and Mirco De Stefani*

My girl sings in her room, alone,
One of the thousand songs she knows
By heart, uploaded sideways on her iPod
Molecule by molecule, soundlessly strung,
Effortlessly flung across innumerable
Times and infinitesimal blue spaces.

So sweet. Her true soprano warbles,
Wobbles, rights itself and then continues on.
Flocks spiraling. How quiet this old house
Will prove in later years, when love
Summons my girl and all the thrushes, starlings,
Finches, doves and waxwings will have flown.

## Canvassing for Mr. Obama

After having draped fifty doorknob hangers
On fifty doors, often without doorknobs,
Some bestraught with pumpkins, some with fierce dogs,
Opened by cheery democrats or slowly,
Silently closed, or slammed, or left ajar:

Blue and scarlet foot-long posters with the words
*Change We Need* beside that thin young man
Barack, Baruch, Blessed, Benedict, meaning the same
Elusive thing in four old languages at odds
Now in the terrible deaf undialectic of war;

I drove back to the election center, radio on,
And suddenly the Jefferson Starship song I once heard
Forty years ago in Grant Park in the spring,
Surrounded by fragrant, pale pink flowering
Cherry trees and dancing children, I heard again.

*If only you believed in miracles, baby,*
*Like I believe, we'd get by;*
*If only you believed like I believe,*
*In miracles, so would I.*

Forty desert years elapsed since politics could
Raise a tear in my dark, disillusioned eye,
But there it was, again. I curbed the car and waited,
Watching light lash through that broken tear, a minor
Flyer for rainbow's contract with the rain.

## What a Poet Wants

If I were a painter, I'd lay gold leaf
On layers of bronze oil paint, glossy leaf-shapes
In wind-dissevered sweeps across the muted canvas.
O my hand, emptied now or almost empty,
Only a brush to ply and a cache of gold
Rapidly disappearing against the grain.

If I were a composer, I'd trace green notes
In long melodic lines like verdigris across the staves,
What the gold-haired, dark-eyed wife must tell her lover,
Once, before she dies in higher registers
And minor keys, the endless harmony
Of love itself an afterthought, an afterlife of sound.

If I were an architect, I'd raise the roof beams
High in flurries of mosaic, genesis or exodus
On Saint Mark's boundless ceiling, crazing the vaults
With everything that moves, fish, flesh and fowl,
Gold on the farmer's pond, the weathered cornfield,
The hill-clouds burnished green in slanting light.

But I am just a poet, given to words,
These slight expressions set on serried pages
One day to flutter from their ribbon bindings,
Friable and lacy as autumn leaves: who will collect them
In some quick human gesture, kissed by a match,
And post them to the house of thoughtlessness?

# December

## Twelfth Night

The Christmas tree is dry:
Resin-dropping twigs whose silky needles
Stroked my hand in Advent, break and crumble.
Time, high time, to take the strung lights down,
The ornaments that shiver,
And from the mantelpiece the gilded star
Beside the homeless family it shone on.

Our house in space is here.
Our house in time is the terrestrial year,
Marked for us by the sun's near disappearance
In night and winter storm,
And those three painted fugitives, who huddle
Against the chill of a wind-riddled byre
To greet a shining baby, small and warm.

# Technical Divination

*For Karine Chemla*

I.
Classical Chinese divining also includes
Possession by a god, but technical methods
Are more widespread and truly more important.

The preferred media, the go-betweens,
Are tortoise shell, whose plates seem to display
A gold cosmography, and yarrow stalks
Cast on a plane. It's reckoning.

In fact, it's the beginning of many methods
For organizing memory: calculi,
Tables with ordered entries,
Series of answered questions, read in runes.

The disposition, studied over and over,
Of stalks on a smooth surface,
May be in fact the origin of rules
For multiplication, and the hexagrams
Of the *I Ching,* which Leibniz learned to cherish.

The questions posed concern
Sanction and prohibition,
Hidden meaning, promising occasion,
Cause and responsibility.

So the virtue of the sage
Is visibly and bodily displayed,
But one must study how to read
His hands and eyes.

II.
There are however other means
Of chatting up or questioning politely
Or forcibly interrogating Fortune.

Track the wind's direction, or the form
And motion of clouds. Record the regular
Movement of heavenly bodies.

Mark anomalous events in heaven:
Comets, eclipses, supernovae, sun storms,
Thunder, lightning, rainbows, promises.

Divination tables may be useful,
And dipper astrolabes that track the Wain
Through lunar lodges, twenty-eight in toto.

Some clouds are shaped like animals;
Some are rainbow tinted, others red,
White, gray, and almost green.

It matters where clouds arise:
Some gather over mountains,
Some are exhaled by rivers or the sea.

Each season has its wind, each wind its music;
Music must be reckoned as a kind
Of tame, intelligent wind.

Dreams too can aid prediction,
Recording where inside and outside *chi*
Clash on the body's battlefield.

With excess *yin,* we dream of fording rivers
In flood; with excess *yang* we dream
Of fires burning cities, burning forests.

With excess *chi* below, we dream of falling;
So we dream of flying
With excess *chi* above, around the heart.

III.
Technical divination
Is not just prophecy for clerks and clerics.

Gods possess the seer in oracles,
Whose voice and consciousness are not her own.

But technical divining's a two-way process
Where each diviner talks back to the gods,

Negotiates, asks them repeated questions
In her own voice and personal awareness.

Thus it bespeaks an attitude toward fate
More like rational persuasion

Than bending before necessity.
God speaks a human idiom

Of dreams and clouds, patterns of wind
And rivers, yarrow stalks that fall,

Segmented years, an empty tortoise shell,
Wandering star-shapes trying to come home.

## The House of Trees

*For Frederick Morgan, in memoriam*

In summer it's a mansion of green rooms
Whose walls of woven honeysuckle border,
Flank of walnut, buttress of wild roses
Enclose the hidden future:
Bleeding heart a sheaf of valentines,
Borage with its litmus-paper-mauve-
To-blue buds set in spiral,
Solomon's seal weighing the fateful options.

But now in winter, weltering snowfall downs
And downy snowdrift, banking up, blow through:
It's all one roofless chamber
Scored by branch and bole, a single upward,
Single outward gesture that composes
Heaven with blue horizon,
And watchman soul sees past the vanished walls
Windows opening on windows opening.

# Justice

*For Christine Clark-Evans and James Stewart*

*"The only purpose for which power can be rightfully exercised over any member of a civilized community against his will is to prevent harm to others."*
—*John Stuart Mill,* On Liberty

This principle is the keystone moral premise
Behind the progressive argument based on justice
That segregated schools, being harmful to children,
Ought thus to be desegregated.

Kenneth B. Clark, a black psychologist,
Devised experiments eighty years ago
In which black children from segregated schools
Played with colored dolls.
When asked to pick "the nice doll," and then again,
"The doll that looks like you,"
More children picked the white doll than the brown.

Clark concluded segregation harmed them.
Clark's experiments, findings, and conclusions
Were largely ignored till 1954, when
Chief Justice Warren in the *Brown* decision
Appealed to those results
As showing, empirically, segregation harms.

Van den Haag dismissed Clark's evidence
As "pseudo-scientific," and Bettelheim
Damned the attempt to base demands for racial
Equity on the data of social science.
Du Bois, the sociologist, who showed
How scientific method clarifies
And proves a just demand, defied them both.

But what is harm? And what is it to prosper?
Fredrick Douglass called the happy man
Virtuous, cosmopolitan, humane,
Autonomous, ruled by reason.
Marcus Garvey called him ruled by race,
Bound by sentiment to group and family.

Booker T. Washington called him enterprising,
Self-reliant, drawn to the marketplace.
Clark agreed with Fanon: it is not justice
To counsel oppressed people to keep their place.
Perhaps a moral distinction guided Clark;
Perhaps his social science was not just science.

A basic education is clearly essential
(As Aristotle argued) to the good life,
Along with reason, and summers of many swallows.
Thus equal opportunity's a notion
Irrelevant to basic education.

Children should not be offered *opportunities*
For education: they aren't free to choose
Not to try to secure one.
Many children apparently make this choice,
But this is intolerable. It must be theirs:
Harm is not having a decent education.

What constitutes a decent education?
Du Bois took vehement issue with Washington
Because, he argued, civic harmony
Cannot depend on money-making alone.
It must be based on respect,
Public acknowledgement of the importance of justice.

Socrates said, true harm is done to the soul
And not the body. Poor, well-educated,
Socrates rarely passed the walls of Athens.
His state made him a philosophical martyr,
Reluctantly and in old age, like Du Bois
Who suffered house arrest
For seven bitter years, then left for Ghana.

Du Bois, who wrote, "The university's function
Is not to teach breadwinning, or how to enter
Polite society. It is, above all else,
To be the organ of that fine adjustment
Between real life and the growing knowledge of life
Which forms the secret of any civilization."

## Holding Pattern

We can't remember half of what we know.
They hug each other and then turn away.
One thinks in silence, never let me go.

The sky above the airport glints with snow
That melts beneath the laws it must obey.
We can't remember half of what we know.

His arms are strong and warm, his breath is slow;
She holds him close, not knowing what to say.
One thinks in silence, never let me go.

Time silts the rivers, ravaging the flow
Of wave on wavelet, and suspends the day.
We can't remember half of what we know.

This holding is agreement to forego,
This flight another strategy to stay.
One thinks in silence, never let me go.

The silver trees spring back to life, although
Their roots are gilded by the leaves' decay.
We can't remember half of what we know,
One thinks in silence. Never let me go.

# January

## Not Summer

It is not summer, and I am not scanning
The peacock feather fan of the Aegean
For one small sailboat, while through plane trees filtering
Sunlight honey-stains the table linen.

No, it is winter, and I sit here writing
In my own quiet bedroom, while outside the forest
Thrums like a gold harp with the unleaving
Wind's performance of its sweet unrest.

# The Warning

*For Eugene Garver and Marc Cogan*

Rhetoric's fairly planned
Strategies for restoring
Values often fall
Foul in the event.
Historians recall
Cicero's tongue and hands
Nailed to the Senate door.

What's the warning? Score
One for Caesar, one
For the translated Sophist.
Patroness of mutes,
A nightingale holds forth
On the Senate roof.
Her trill is ominous.

"Better speak than yield
To silence; and yet better
Speak with your tongue
Still fastened to your head.
Who needs more dead
Eloquence, or tight-lipped
Republican emperors?"

## Days of 1983

I came to visit you, but only slightly,
Like sunlight from the east when break of day
Chases the dream clouds over the horizon,
Glimpsed from a certain angle, half recalled.

Four or five days, no more, arriving only
After you'd shut the door and hid the key
Under the terra-cotta pot of basil,
And rushed off to your airplane, late as usual.

I used up all the maté in the tin
And found it always made my heart beat faster;
I played your Dvořák tapes, the older tangos,
And sang along with *Tosca,* start to finish,

Though as you know I strongly disapprove
Of firing squads, and death by parapet.
You'll find some new Rossini tapes, and Mozart,
And Motown, waiting for you on the table

Whose legs are, incidentally, very wobbly.
I hope you'll learn some other songs by heart
And bracket the table legs: I'd do it for you,
But carpentry is not my cup of maté.

Besides, what kind of store sells nails and brackets?
I found the grocery store, but had no time
To learn the odd taxonomy of commerce.
Most of my hours I spent in your soft chair

Reading, of course, and listening to the quarrels
Of neighbors, cats, whatever it is you call
Those little birds who always seem so hungry.
I must say I especially enjoyed

Sleeping on your pillow, between your sheets
While they still smelled like you, until the older
Lady who cleans your house changed all the linens.
Each day at nightfall, I walked the few blocks

To your train-station café, and drank some coffee
Watching the light drift under the horizon,
Writing these dream notes down to tuck beside
The key, beneath the fragrant pot of basil.

You'll see me turn the corner as you turn
The corner, coming home, a flash of heels
And pocketbook and scarlet flowered silk;
An optical illusion; a trace of tears.

I left some roses, but I fear they're fading
As Ronsard says they will, or just unsung
As Borges says they are. I left my scent
(Chanel), and I refilled your tin of maté.

# On Painting

*For Farhad Ostovani*

I.
Bihzad in his white suit,
In snow-white light across
The window facing Hághia Sophía,
As though he'd long ago become
A spirit in the Otherworld.

"Ah, Tiflis!" the great master sighed,
Gazing at the light that glowed,
That seemed to glow,
From the snow-covered garden.
"In Tiflis, is it snowing now?"

II.
Painting is the silence of thought,
And the music of sight.

III.
As a tree, I only grow, and breathe.
As a picture, though, I grieve
Because I'm not a page in some bright book
Hand-lettered, catalogued, and bound in leather.

The reason for my loneliness is this:
I'm not sure where I go.
I was supposed to be an episode,
But then I fluttered down, an autumn leaf.

IV.
Like the mind of God, who sees
And understands all things:
Exhibit the underside.

The pith beneath the bark,
The castle in cross-section,
The human hearth, the furniture, the cause.

V.
When it snows, soft down
Makes light of Tiflis keep,
Pillows the fortress walls.
The washerwoman sings
Rose-colored verses, girls
Hide ice cream underneath
Their feather beds, a sweet
Frozen midsummer dream.

VI.
Study to return
To darkness by the sidelong path of color.

VII.
A teaspoonful of pale rose-petal jam.
Lamb stew in sauce
Heavy with beaten eggs,
Spiced with sour plum.
A compote of stewed figs.
Fresh bread. Wine.

VIII.
Before the art of painting there was darkness,
And afterward the darkness will return.
To know is to remember what you've seen.
To see is knowing without memory.
Thus, painting is remembering the darkness.

## The Kitchen Window

*For Cinda Agnew Musters (Amsterdam, 2004)*

Your kitchen's in the basement, dark on winter mornings
But never cold, stocked with the impromptu riches you cull
Daily from markets along the canals, flower-strewn
Even in winter, when streetlamps have to kindle early
And gleam in gathering mist, shine on folding water.

How often, Cinda, I've sought refuge in your long line
Of beautiful, composed houses, and watched you ahead of me
Join the endlessly complicated fray of raising children.
Outside your kitchen window, beyond the sunken garden,
We see the tree Anne Frank recorded from her attic room.

The neighborhood contributes to its preservation,
Watching anxiously from kitchen windows, as its bole
Hollows, balds, leans more heavily on the big crutches.
Once it showed Anne Frank the seasons she could not touch,
And she recorded them. Our children read the leaves.

# February

## No Moon

October's gone. No golden moon tonight
Flooding the still lush foliage in the woods
Behind my house, black walnut, oak, and maple.

Now the trees are empty, and the moon is white,
Just half a face, a lover turned away
Like Dido in the shadow realm of Hades.

# Forsythia

*For Cinda (Philadelphia, 1964)*

Every spring, when the bright yellow, starry flutes of forsythia
Suddenly burst out from the dull monotones that are all February
And March can muster, always the same lilting ostinato, always
The same and always a surprise,

I'm back in my home town, walking under the shadows of the overpass,
Under the Main Line train tracks and the Japanese pavilion-station
With its carved wooden dragons left over from the World's Fair only
My grandparents remembered,

And so now of course no one, past the haunted mansion parenthesized by
Weeping beeches, where I recall the revenant who sank into an armchair
But only the chair was visible, past the Revolutionary War cemetery
With its tilted, sunken gravestones

Carved in a lovely archaic script that no one now can decipher,
Past my aunt's house that has been repainted and replanted, where
I learned all I know about classical music by listening to my uncle
Play Liszt, Beethoven, Chopin,

To your house, Cinda, where you watched from the plate-glass window
With your tennis racket and towel, ready to join me in a melodic assault on
The park court where we improvised, chasing and losing the bright tonic
Of tennis ball and sharp intention,

In those days when the sky was perfectly blue and throbbed in unison
With the gold wind section of forsythia, and our limbs answered to reason,
And we could run for hours without considering, stopped only finally
By the dark *scherzo* of sundown.

# Morning Delivery of *The Times*

*For Ruth Fainlight*

I went out to look for the newspaper,
But the driveway was empty,
And behind the dark trees
Dawn was turning the sky-vault
Champagne-shot blue silk,
A backdrop with roses.
Who was it for?
There were no voices or music,
Only a woodpecker's thrum.
Somewhat confused, I withdrew
And went back inside.

I went out again
To look for the damned newspaper,
Because I had nothing to read
With my coffee.
But the driveway was still empty,
And behind the dim house
Frozen cushions of moss
Gleamed like a green velvet
Ball gown embroidered with crystals.
Who was dancing?
I couldn't tell, so I went back inside.

I went out again and discovered,
At the edge of the ballroom, a slight
Cotillion of snowdrops, dancing
Although they'd been covered completely
By blizzards, twice.
And after I bowed to the flowers
In admiration, I turned
And there at the foot of the driveway,
Much like a scrap of snow,
Or a speckled, swan-feather fan,
Lay the newspaper.

## While You Lay Sleeping

Sometimes when I wake up in the small hours,
Roused by the moon whose slow mercurial beams
Insinuate themselves across my eyes,
Or dreams, or hunger, or some unaccomplished
Task, or errant children far from home,
I hear you snoring like a warm volcano:
Clouds drape your shoulders like the basalt slopes
Of Fuji I glimpsed almost a month ago,
Although that vision from the Bullet Train's
Strait windows was intangible and cold,
But beautiful. I touch your shoulder blade,
Gently, so you roll over on your side
And snores turn into regular sweet breathing,
The up-and-down, the in-and-out of time,
Composing underchords of lullaby
So, tuned and comforted, I fall asleep.

*Ut musica pictura*

*Farhad Ostovani, Iris Noir (2008)*

The flower stem leans sideways as it fades.
The curling leaves are brownish, burnt by time,
But here and there a color, olive-gray or lime,
Shines out: a pane, a memory of green.

Across the antique paper, lately saved
From fire or dustbin when the engraver closed
His now outmoded studio: year and number,
And then a sideways crease, scored by a century.

So paper has a memory, like flowers.
So too the artist, who still keeps his iris
Dark by the sunlit window, that he painted
Over and over many months ago. And see,

Not just the picture but his sketches, trace
Of two ghost flowers he didn't draw, and left
Beside the one he did: magenta, purple, orange.
Trace of the artist's hand. And then the date.

## Snowdrop

Snow fell so early this year, just after Allhallows,
We never finished the ritual of raking clean
Livid grass and cushions of stricken moss.
The yard's still matted with leaves, oak, maple, walnut,
Visible once again as the snow recedes,
Tatted lace unravelling, going wherever the snows
Of yesteryear retire to, heaven or hellward.
Under the mat of crisscrossed mahogany
And black gold crusted with ice, one snowdrop rises.

She stands already in the outmost bed, bordering
Woods, though it is only February, turned,
Dear Mary-Frances, less than a week ago. I laid
The coverlet of leaves aside and there she was,
Furled on herself and bowed, but blooming hard,
Sober, exquisite child of an uncertain season.

# Elegy

*For Maxine Kumin, in memoriam*

On February first, I went outside
Stepping through pot-cheese snow to look for sprouts,
And there they were,
The tiny dark green tips of snowdrop spears.

I took a snapshot with my pocket camera,
Intending to print it up
And send it north as I do every year
To let you know that spring is coming soon,
A little earlier here than it arrives
At your New England farm
Perched high against the hillside, house and barn,
Vegetable patch and meadows and dark pond.

Now it is April. February, March
Were lost to ice-storms, blizzards, inland squalls,
And those small stunted sprouts
Could only freeze and unfreeze, freeze again
And wait till April broke: now here they are.
But you were lost before I had a chance
To send your picture north.

Now I could send you flowers,
Dozens of snowdrops starting up in wreaths,
And next to them the striped and dimly starred
And gilded crocuses,
And fast behind the budding daffodils—
Phallic, I think you'd say,
Pleased by the blunt irreverence of saying:
Upward! Inverse to scrota dangling down,
Those metaphoric green beans in your garden.

They're blooming anyway and everywhere!
And where are you? Who should be here to meet them,
To cast your practiced eye
On my unkempt, unprincipled backyard,
And on this poem that I might have sent
Except I wrote it down because you're gone.

## Counterpane

*For Maxine Kumin, in memoriam, and for Irene Harvey*

Boomer, daughter of Taboo,
Dam of Hallelujah, and
Earlier of Praise Be,
Today lies under snow,
Her coverlet precisely
Quilted by the hand
Of February and her kind
Owners, over many years,
In Rail Fence pattern,
Except for one edge where
A bright celestial neighbor
Adds a square: North Star.

# March

## Spring Cleaning

This season's a disaster: autumn leaves
Still cram the hidden, blind interstices
Bushes subtend between the house and lawn,
Between our property and someone else's,
Crawl spaces tunneled intermittently
By rabbit, squirrel, and children, who emerge
Crusted with twigs and pill bugs.
And underfoot the glint of broken toys.

And overall the new leaves burgeoning
And branches downed and gelid daffodils
That bloomed and froze,
Volunteer bluets cornering the grass,
Plaited mouse and chipmunk, what remains
Of barn owl night thoughts, crooked, undigested.
Bleached or blackening beside the leaf pile,
One heap of sticks like vertebrae or ribs.

Weltering, paratactic, adjectival:
A great unseemly biomass, here and there
And neither here nor there. Too much for me,
Who should by now have set the leaf meal curbside
In conical matched sets fit for the vacuum
Cleaner truck, and racks of leafless sticks
For the great mulcher, with its gloved and goggled
Ministers, that seals the fate of spring.

# Two Meditations on Stone

*For Donald Davie, in memoriam*

### Montreux

And there beyond the tended paths
And flower borders shadowed by the lamps
Of white magnolia, pear, camellia, plum,
Beyond the grand hotels and chocolate shops,

Across the lake, the gods.
Silent, near, their hair marbled with snow,
The gods stare downward as if lost in thought,
But what their judgments are, we never know.

### Rome

There it stands, the Pantheon,
The same as ever: shallow dome,
Pillars shouldering the pediment
Which for millennia declared
*Agrippa fecit.* So
Stand the Colosseum,
Titus' Arch and Constantine's,
The Wall Aurelian raised:
Waiting, it seems, for us
When we return at last.

But look at those blank faces,
The eyeless brow, the hand,
The flank, the granite ledge.
Though we recall each splendid
Ostinato, what they stood for
Fifty years ago, or
Twenty centuries, our great
Progenitors in stone
Cannot remember us,
Or chasten, or forget.

## What I Forgot, What I Could Not Forget

Three in the morning. Panicked, I wake up
And think, I can't forget to bring the camera!
Passport, paper, face cream, extra shoes.
At dawn, I pack up everything except
The first thing I remembered, and head east.

The steep hills of Jerusalem reproach me.
Cypress heavy with fruit even in winter,
Cyclamen, feral cats, the golden limestone
Walls of the Old City, the Valley of Hell
Deep in its streamless vale, a burnished sky.

The Church of the Dormition plants its spire
White-gold against the blue of heaven, that warms
A garden copse of tiny, sweet-skinned oranges.
No photographs. And yet the hidden contours,
The heft, the shadow tones, remain and burn.

## Leaving the Garden

Ruins are traces. Discourse on the rainbow:
Optics rewritten as a science not
Of light rays nor of images, but shadows.

For there are certain passions of the light
Illuminating, altering the screens,
The *camera oscura,* of the eye.

The eye itself incapable of vision.
Go calculate the angles of refraction,
As fountains make the rainbow visible,

Fountains and prisms, vapors, vestiges.
For God has left his mark upon the world,
The glory of the shadows. Stamp and seal.

## Goodbye to State College

"I liked the way the light came in the windows
Of our old house," says William. "I remember
It filtered through the trees; we had so many trees!"
Maple, birch, black walnut, dogwood, redbud
And lots of weedy oaks loaded with acorns.

"The morning light made leaf prints on the kitchen wall...."
And Dutch lace scallops up and down the hallway
Beside your uncle's uncle's watercolors
Of Paris gardens and the Gare d'Orsay,
Beyond your parents' decorated bedroom

Where you were made one day in February
When squall and sunlight dazzled icicles in rows
And snow quilted the forest with its silent citizens,
Bear, red squirrel, chipmunk, groundhog, hidden,
And bold apparent jays and cardinals on the branches.

"Sunset light was also level sideways..."
And threw the rhododendrons up in rosy silhouettes
Beside your great-grandmother's student sketches
Of plaster casts of goddesses with Roman noses
And one Japanese lady in kimono.

"Forty trees around the house!" Another sixty set behind us
In a thick copse, where your distracted mother
Would look for crocuses and snowdrops in the spring
And warily for a sleeping bear who might wake up
Hungry and fierce, with cubs, bedecked with flowers.

# April

## April 7, 2011

*For my cousin, Trish Grosholz Burchardt*

A cool, gray, bitter spring day
Chases me out to the farm roads,
Where some sweet racket arrests me
By a brake of leafless trees
Shielding the wrecked cornfields.

Look: a flock of migrant robins,
Their warm chests puffed out
Against the sharpening wind, as if
The trees were full of apricots,
And apricots could sing and fly away.

# On Pilgrim Hill

*For Paula Deitz*

On Pilgrim Hill, where New York City rises
Above itself, a grove of cherry trees
Donated by Japan surrounds the cast-iron,
Buckled and hatted statue. Just at sunset

We walk there, you and I and Mary-Frances,
To see them blossoming, and then because
That moment is so brief, to watch as well
The fair beginning of their downfall,

Not a rain of petals. From these fruitless trees
The flowers tumble altogether, pale corollas,
Pentagonal snowflakes, rafts that twirl and ride
Currents of the air, downdraft to lakeside

Where Mary-Frances charms the waterbirds:
A thin blue heron spreads his wings for her,
Brushing a wayward blossom as it strays
In reverie to the mirror of a wave.

In reverie, you talk of other days
That somehow ended and somehow abide.
How often you walked past here with your husband,
Idling on a park bench, lost in conversation, found.

*Strange*, you say, and look across the clouds.
*One day last week I stood here, and a passing*
*Gentleman I didn't see, not pausing,*
*Paid me a compliment. He said, you are*

*The best dressed woman in the park, my dear.*
And Mary-Frances spirals back, translucent feather
Lifted on the upswing, interrupting, so then neither
Says what we both think: a messenger.

## The Beautiful Game

I.
Forces unexpected, untoward sweep
Up and down the field at cheetah speed,
Wind speed, indeed sometimes the dervish turbine
Of victory-defeat seems to spin round
Faster than sound, or light, and therefore time.
Stars racing away from me, then racing home.

Lion rounding antelope, gazelle eluding
Sudden night beneath the leopard's paw
Printed with stars, that mortal circulation
Tracks the green pitch as if turf were veldt,
Kilimanjaro veiled in muslin snow
Where I stand by, all eyes, watching the clouds

Dousing the sunlight shining here and there
Against the players as they track the ball,
Feint, block, fill up the spaces on the field where
Offense and defense meld like sun and shadow.
How does the match turn out? I never know,
Win, lose or draw, the way my children dazzle.

II.
Along the edges of the soccer pitch
The maple trees are coming into focus.
Shoals of coral lace, or islands in the air
Whose gradients are differential flowers
Too fine to see against the upper branches.
My son commands the center of the field.
His boots are yellow and his shirt is silver.
We're down two-one, the sun sets in the corner

And turns the same light color as the trees.
Eleven on a side. I want my child
To win, but he is one soul among many,
And I am just his mother, sunstruck, silent,
Tracking shifts of wind, or luck, or mind
Beneath the drifting russet-argent. *Goal.*

III.
Driving my black-eyed son to a tournament
Where he'll show off his striking physical brilliance,
Moving the soccer ball as the wind shifts sand
To fashion a sinusoidal wave-edge over dunes,
I notice the emerald hills of Pennsylvania
Silent beneath a Sunday afternoon.
How smooth the hills are, polished, almost flawless.

But wait! Beneath that seamless green illusion
A thousand deer are moving, a myriad squirrels
Rake the earth for walnuts, the dim earth stirred
By a million earthworms frothing the under-matrix.
And mountain laurel blossoms burst into whiteness
And rhododendrons mauve, distraught by bees;
Ferns unfurl and violets fold their lanceolate leaves.

And all the oaks, wild apples, dogwoods, locusts
Breathe our excess, stale excrescence, deeply in
And out sweet rolling waves of air. O hills,
So like my hand posed briefly on the dashboard,
Beneath whose steep abysm a billion billion
Billion carbon atoms skitter under the flail
Across that bright invisible threshing floor.

# Mind

*For Hourya Benis Sinaceur*

The enormous, high-ceilinged apartment near Trocadéro
Echoes, though it is full of books, intaglio'd furniture, and flowers,
As if reflecting the old house in Rabat, now seized and lost,
And the great, oceanless dunes ranged beyond the city walls
That bear the trace of wind sifting, but not of mind.

You write the history of mind, entering its formal labyrinth
With only the silk thread of demonstration to lead you on.
So Hilbert guides you, Poincaré, Weyl, Noether, Cavaillès.
So Emmy Noether grieved for Hilbert's house, her home and circle,
Stranded on the outskirts of Philadelphia, where she died.

So Göttingen fell, the greatest commonwealth of mind
Europe ever knew, dismantled by the agents of the Reich
Who sized up living mathematicians as Catholics, women, Jews.
So Cavaillès was shot against a wall, so Emmy Noether,
Exiled from her algebraic home, succumbed to memory. *Don't you.*

# Leaves and Clouds

*For Roberta Caplan*

In modern life, where friends dispersed so seldom meet,
Doing something twice becomes tradition: ours is
Swimming in your quiet neighborhood pool, tandem,
Plying the backstroke, gazing up at clouds and leaves.

Where's your mother now? Dispersed in leaves and clouds
As we glide underneath them, arm over arm over arm,
Trying to stay afloat, look lively, raise our children.
The last time I saw Libby, I drove my aunt to meet her,

From the Christian to the Jewish suburbs of Philadelphia.
I had to leave home to meet you, Roberta, though you and I
Lived parallel child-lives not ten miles away from each other;
Libby and Anna would never have met in the old dispersion.

I stopped at a florist, and loaded the car with stargazer lilies,
Clouds of baby's breath, roses, mums: a flowery comment on
Two dear souls with an almost unlimited gift for affection
And funny stories aimed at those who tried the limits.

Readers, fabulous hostesses, ever-loving mothers,
They recognized one another for what they were and talked
For hours. We drew the curtains to gaze at Libby's garden,
And then the room was full of laughter, leaves and clouds.

## Where I Went, and Cannot Come Again

That crabapple tree is gone, that used to blossom, no,
To burst like a low budget, pale pink Vesuvius
Halfway between our back door and the neighbors'
Who spoke Italian when the dark-eyed grandmothers appeared.

So too the ash, whose canopy embowered, overshadowed
The lawn with lunar-eclipse shadows, and the small magnolia
Whose open flowers filled up like bowls of alabaster
With April rain, their lips rimmed gold with pollen.

The dogwood's gone I used to climb, the sailor's mast
Blue spruce that lifted almost to the rooftop,
Even the wind-stunted Japanese pine that slanted
Sideways to shelter daylilies, marigolds and tulips.

Even the late-planted holly bush, that lent an air
Of Christmas to the suite of rhododendrons
That screened the front door, and the Christmas trees
Planted year by year against the uproar of the Lincoln highway.

All of them are gone now, and the house is bare,
Mere office space for the adjacent Catholic parish.
Mother, where's the garter snake once hidden in violets,
Periwinkle, hyacinth, all of them blue, all scattered?

Father, where's the porch you built and screened, each nail
Carefully marked and measured in blue pencil? Where's the girl
Who used to slam those doors in helpless anger, and returns
Now to name the vanished trees and close, more gently, the
   unopened doors?

# May

## Not Roses

Not roses beside the stately homes of England
I frequent now to study the ancient science
Of horticulture, back to the Italians,
Moors, and Persians, alchemist-gardeners
Who coaxed that whorl of damask petals upward
From five to dozens, hundreds,
Thousands, like the kisses of Catullus.

But riotous unclaimed orchids, long ago
On the great upland chessboard of Lasithi,
And Queen Anne's lace like snowy inverse shadows
Around the redbud trees that overwhelm
The tumbled columns of Olympia,
And wild geraniums massed along the highways
Between Siena and the gates of Rome.

# Uncertain

> "Someone who, dreaming, says 'I am dreaming,' even if he speaks audibly in doing so, is no more correct than if he said in his dream, 'It is raining,' while in fact it was raining. Even if his dream were actually connected with the sound of the rain."
> —The final lines of Ludwig Wittgenstein's On Certainty

Four o'clock: still night and silence.
I hear one local bird practice a trill,
Then silence falls again.
Why did it sing?

Are birds like us misled
By false dawn? By a dream
Of moonrise? Ever roused, eye-struck
By rays of moonlight?

We cannot say its song
Was caused by the moon rising,
Even if it dreamed
The moon, as the moon rose.

In any case, darkness prevails.
A mystery, unless I too
Dreamed the bird, its trill, the pale
Ruse of moonlight.

# Insomnia

Startled from dreams, anxious, I glance outside
To check if that pale glare across your window
Signals you're still awake. But wait, you've gone
Back to your summer job, just yesterday.

Earth and the green horizon curve. From here,
I can't discern Manhattan, that great bright
Ocean liner moored to its granite dock, held
Fast for an aeon, tugged by the gray Atlantic.

There is your modest cabin, storeys up,
Perched on the northwest corner. Is your light
Still on? Or rocking on that rise and swell,
The hawser'd city-ship, are you asleep?

# Two Passages from Colette

*For Sheila Malovany-Chevallier and Constance Borde*

I.

For I already loved daybreak so much that my mother would give it to me as a reward. I got her to wake me up at three-thirty in the morning, and I set out with an empty basket on each arm toward the little market gardens hidden in the narrow loop of the river, toward the strawberries, the currants, and the bearded gooseberries.

At three-thirty, everything lay asleep in the blue of genesis, humid and vague, and as I walked down the sandy path, the mist—landlocked by its own weight—bathed first my legs, then my sturdy little torso, finally rising to my lips, my ears, and my nostrils, all of them more sensitive than the rest of my body.... I went alone, this free-thinking countryside held no dangers.

It was on this path and at this hour that I became aware of my own worth, of an ineffable state of grace and of my own complicity with the first breeze that stirred, the first bird, the sun once again oval, distorted by its blossoming on the horizon....

My mother let me go, after having called me "Beauty, Jewel-all-of-gold"; she watched her *chef-d'œuvre,* as she called me, run off and disappear down the slope of the garden. I was perhaps pretty; my mother and pictures of me at that time do not always yield the same judgment....

But I was pretty at that moment, because of my age and because day was dawning, because of my blue eyes made somber by the shadows of foliage, and my tousled hair that would not be smoothed down until my return, and my childish sense of superiority, to be awake before all those other sleeping children.

I returned when the church bells announced the first mass. But not before having eaten my fill, not before having described a great circuit in the woods like a dog out hunting by himself, not before having drunk at two hidden springs which I worshipped....

II.

The little girl, tired out, mechanically repeats, "When I shall travel around the world..." as if she were saying, "When I shall go shake chestnuts from the trees...."

A spot of red lights up inside the house, behind the windows of the sitting room, and the little girl starts.

Everything that was green an instant before has become blue, around that red, immobile flame.

The child's hand, trailing in the grass, senses the dew of evening. It is the hour of lamps.

The lapping sound of running water rises in the leaves; as if by a wintry gust, the door of the hayloft begins to bang against the wall.

The garden, all at once hostile around the sobered little girl, brushes back the cold leaves of the laurel, flourishes the sabers of the yucca and the barbed caterpillars of the araucaria.

A great oceanic voice groans from the direction of the Moûtiers where the wind, unobstructed, runs in gusts over the swell of the woods.

The little girl in the grass fixes her eyes on the lamp, which a brief eclipse has just veiled: a hand has passed in front of the flame, a hand that wears a shining thimble.

## Just a Star

An olive tree can live a thousand years,
Drawing its silver leaves and oval fruit
From stony terraces, fretting the wind
In registers of sun-inflected shadow.

But we, my love, who count the terraces
Rising to meet the stories of the sky,
Who cultivate the olive groves, who hear
The interruption in the trees as music

And weep responsive to those minor chords,
Can live only a century, no more.
Although I love you, you are just a man,
And the great silver sun is just a star.

# June

## Silver

Beside the road I took, another road
Winds under trees that never grow
Across the long, low hills of Pennsylvania:
Eucalyptus, date palm, casuarina.
The absent sea falls underneath the moon.

Beside a grove of olive trees
The lost wind silvers, cypresses that bend
And lean into the sun, another road
Climbs up a hill behind the distant river,
Turns under a sheaf of roofs, and disappears.

## The Art of Glassblowing

Rolling the hollow tube, the great baton
Through which he breathes a form into the vase,
The *souffleur de verre* leans into his design,
The almost liquid globe of molten glass.

Behind him in the furnace the fire roars,
A thousand degrees Celsius and climbing,
So bright behind the open iron doors
He cannot look inside. It is a wing.

It is a flower, a crown, a fallen apple,
A shawl of snow, a comber on the sand
That thins. Desire bent to principle,
The flux of Heraclitus brought to mind.

# Elliptic Curves and Modular Forms Converge South of the Taklamakan

*For Wen-Ch'ing (Winnie) Li*

A skein of silk amid the iron and bronze weapons,
The trade routes brought my number theory teacher, Dr. Li,
Who writes faster with white chalk on the blackboard
Than any human being I ever followed across a proof,
Raising clouds of chalk dust at the furrowed extremities
Of each long expedition toward a theorem. Camels
Cough and huddle by the caravansary, in moonlight.

I carry cough drops with me in my book bag, under notes,
So I won't interrupt her train of thought by sneezing,
And try to copy every line she writes, as well as those
Brief detours on heuristics, or her mild evaluations
Of depth or usefulness or interest of conjectures, placed
Unexpectedly like waterfalls down clefts in limestone,
Or her infrequent, offhand explanations of the way
She generalized a printed remark of Serres, from gamma-
Zero-$p$ ($p$ prime, indexing groups of matrices) to any level.

How algebraic form can complement the smooth analysis
That frames the proof, the complex upper half-plane poised
Like some great violet dome on whose connected face
The primes come out, appearing one by one in constellations
Above the Taklamakan Desert where the Silk Route ran
From Xian, between the winding Yellow River and the great
But perished Wall, to break against the lovely gates of Kashgar.

## Primary School

My four children learned to read here, to talk back
And repent in the principal's office, to unlock
The ivory puzzle-box of the multiplication tables,
To utter a few lovely phrases of Japanese,
To marry and give birth and die in imaginary
Covered wagons laboring from St. Louis to Sacramento.

Today my daughter read an essay to the assembly,
And my youngest son played a Mozart air on his fiddle.
So for the last time I visited their first school, Easterly,
Namesake perhaps of the morning star, that shines
Only a little while before and after dawn, though secretly
It is also the evening star, and the errant planet Venus.

Fourteen years under this tangle of elm trees, lindens,
Black walnuts, pin oaks that rust bronze in October,
Maples that launch their bright wings downward in April.
I wrote my name on a paper badge marked "visitor,"
And kept it afterward, as if it might somehow later
Reopen the doors, sealed now by the guardian of years.

# The Stars of Earth

*For my children, and my brother Rob Grosholz*

Come away, come outside *now,* we whispered to the children
Who, that summer's night, were plastered to the noisy screen
Of their electric muses, cell phone, television, texting, Word.
They tumbled from their couches anyway, half-roused, and followed

Blindly across the street and up the hill beside the churches,
Far to the edge of cornfields, looking down the valley's darkness
And farther away the darkness of uneven glacial hills, moraine
Fashioned fifty thousand years ago, years when there was no summer.

Darkness everywhere, and four awed children shivering in the warmth,
And as we turned back home, we came to a tree on fire with fireflies,
A veteran oak encrusted from crown to root with tiny disturbances
That pulsed and blazed as if they sang of love, but sang in silence.

# July

## Here and There

What will I miss when I'm gone?
The squeak of the wheelbarrow's wheel,
Grace note that strikes with every slow
Revolution, and then the hushed, rusty
Answer in triplets from the invisible
Bird in the lackluster maples.

Branches, weeds, last autumn's leavings
Raked from the moss-eaten paths, beds,
Borders, still untrimmed hedges.
Also the silent pale blue bells
Of my half dozen borage, ringed,
Self-seeded from the woods.

Daylilies my mother liked to set
Roadside in June. Pale Greek anemones
She never traveled far enough
To find wild, as I did once or twice, but
Maybe I'll bring her some, if over there
Windflowers blow beside a cloudy sea.

# Sunset

*For Regina Glaess and Patience Thouin*

The baby splashes down in the wading pool
Like a fluffed sparrow landing in a birdbath:
Droplets everywhere, and cries of pleasure,
And feathers! Her big sister notices at last
And quits her storybooks to join the half-
Prism, half-fountain crimsoned in the long
Northern sunset cast across Westphalia.
Their grandmother presides,
Disposing cake and coffee near the lindens.

But wait, that's you! A little thinner and grayer,
Yet still the same tall figure I recall when
You were Mama, your girl the bright fledgling,
And all your letters shimmered with adventure.
Don't those children know you watched the moon rise
Over the Finnish tundra, over Saharan dunes,
And single-handed fought the great mist-dragons
That guard Victoria Falls
Before misfortune closed Zimbabwe's borders?

# Citizens

*For Jackie Dee King*

Here we are again, by Cape Cod's involuted shoreline,
Looking out past pines and sea grass where, on the shimmering cove,
Catboats and schooners sail past at intervals, and a red-tailed hawk
Lands on the high island of a pine crown, and preens for the camera.

Fifty years ago, it was only another beach, an occasion
For getting tan, meeting cute boys, parrying waves, dozing,
Reading romantic novels. Now we herd our children before us
With some anxiety, and bring our binoculars and field guides.

We know now that in four thousand years Cape Cod will vanish;
Global warming might even accelerate the lapse. It's only
A remnant, a spit of sand already gently eroding its beachfronts
Though real estate agents buy and sell as if there were no tomorrow.

All the same, we hold to the things we've learned, and teach our children:
Heaps of sea grass are food and shelter for littoral creatures
And shouldn't be tidied up; some clusters of shells are porches
For highly constructed tube-worm homes; the moon creates the tides.

The beach is not a theater, the globe's no Globe, despite what
Shakespeare's Prospero said, for we are citizens, not actors.
So we go down again, with our real children and our novels
Understood otherwise, and spread our towels across the sand,
And talk, and track the red-tailed hawk who settles against moonrise.

# Astronomy

*Gunnison Valley Observatory, Colorado*

*For Gordon Fleming and Frederick Turner*

The empty page reproaches me
Like the blue sky devoid of clouds,
The sun's diffuse, refracted light
Hiding ten thousand visible stars
And, further off, a hundred billion
Galaxies our eyes will never see,
Redshifting as they leave us, waving goodbye.

Goodbye, goodbye. I can't recall
Their names sometimes; sometimes their names
Come back to me: Vega, Aldebaran.
Sometimes a lucky telescope extends
Up from a cleft observatory dome
Perched on the high plains, ringed about
By berms and mountains: then the stars appear.

Look! There are the rings of Saturn,
Horns, and there are craters on the moon,
And seas that are not seas, and there,
Oh, look! a double star that peers
Like fox eyes from the den of space.
And there's a spiral galaxy, all arms.
And here's the poem, burning on the page.

## Kisses

What is the magic of lips?
Almost anyone will shake your hand:
That warm press of flesh on flesh bespeaks
A common heat or grace,
Willingness to bury long complaint,
Ill will, injustice under a civil act
Where grass can grow.

We hug our friends, sometimes
Colleagues on a consequential day,
Even utter strangers if
Events rain down on us by way of
Grief or celebration.
And lips occasionally brush hands
To signify an honorable homage.

But lips on lips! Ah, then
The world-magician turns us inside out:
Heaven descends as rain,
Rivers catch fire, fire
Separates flame by flame by flame
To rainbow so the *arc-en-ciel*
Fleetingly gilds and binds the shattered world.

# Equal and Opposite

*For Jean Starobinski*

Reaction is the movement that cannot resign itself.
It is not just a tool, it is a task. The writer must react!
Reaction is the spurring of resistance,
Invention of response.

Knowing only what opposes us, uncertain how to manifest refusal
And overcome Goliath—so inexplicable, unjust, ungoverned—
The writer somehow refuses to consent
To things as they stand.

The writer must react: this is a Kantian imperative, a duty,
Yet indeterminate. A warning in the wake of evident danger
That comes without the guarantees of theory
Or promise of success.

Reaction is above all personal, written—enacted in speech—
By individuals facing impersonal forces, who must answer
Although we see now as through a glass
Darkly, not face to face.

The writer sets to work not knowing what will finally emerge
From personal reactions, aiming only for admissible response,
Between a past whose meaning is a riddle,
And a half-hidden future.

We hope to find the causes that make us live, but it is we ourselves
Who look for our beginnings. We are the origin of the long search
For origins, and poetry is always the imitation
Of human action.

# August

## Daylilies

Here and there along the country roads
Only a few daylilies remain, sentinels
Posted to the frontiers of an empire
Whose capital city has already fallen.

## Letter from Châtel-Montagne

Along the road that leads beyond the village,
Behind the church, late afternoon sun warms
A great stone wall. Among the coral bells
Lit by its passage, tiny hummingbirds
No larger than the frequent fat black bees
Hover and shimmer, trying to drink their fill
Though they are never satisfied. How small
Their nests must be, woven inside the grass.

When we return, evening has cooled the stone
And closed the bells. The hummingbirds are gone.
My son observes, their wings beat thirty times
A second, but the miracle described
Must fail to conjure them, and the frail flowers
Avert their gaze. Silence is evensong.
It is too late to show you what I mean,
Writing only with words from Châtel-Montagne.

## Abbey Road

There is a small green-urban grocery store
With mums and dahlias (browned) and crimson-orange
Strawberries, clementines, tomatoes, carrots.
A linden tree just finishing its flower
Perfumes the air and spatters the damp pavements.
Windows disguise a hundred private dramas
And pigeons on the roofs crest chimney pots
That once presided over household fires.

The day-sky threatens, yet it doesn't rain;
The summer wind is cold. Where are the songs
Of spring, that use to play when I was young?
Keats claims I have my music too, or still,
But one sweet song has died, and one lies ill,
And two are stalked by failure, pain and fear.

## The Tallinn Ferry

The ferryboat from Helsinki to Tallinn
Passes small islands into the open sea,
The Baltic. Brackish, neither sweet nor salt,
It plays congenial host to microscopic
Flora and fauna flourishing only here.
Only here. The sunset shines behind us
And lights the northern dome of heaven slantwise
As if dusk were midday, which it is,
Almost, in summer near the Arctic Circle.

This boat reminds me of another ferry
I boarded more than forty years ago,
From Brindisi to Patras. A southern sea
With the same perfect circle at the edges
Thanks to our finite eyes, the curvature
Of almost perfect earth, that oblate sphere,
The same slate blue at evening, but another
Dark-eyed man was waiting on the shore,
Hidden behind the folded wing of years.

For hours there is nothing on the horizon.
It's just a circle, as the river of time
Is just a line: fixed banks or flowing stream?
The line withholds its secrets, like the circle.
Then gleams arise, the facets of a cliff,
The windows of a city, the shimmer of ships
Moored close together round a crescent harbor.
And so my vanished loves sometimes appear
At sunset, as the ferry veers toward home.

## European Paper

It is a little narrower, a little thicker,
And longer, so the edges in my folder
Get slightly creased from sticking past the bounds
Fixed by American convention: ten plus one
Inches down and eight point five across.
So one can sometimes add two or three lines
Before the poem stalls against the trim
Implacable horizon of Page End.

Ah, Fates. Before I finally come home,
Back to the realm of wider, shorter, thinner,
Back to the rules that both constrict and comfort,
Grant me a brief extension on the page:
Seagulls gleaming past the ferryboat's long wake,
The cliffs of Tallinn silver gilt at midnight.

## Yesterday

Yesterday it was still summer, the farmer's fields
Brimming with soy and corn, and along the edges where
We walked, talking of time, *Remembrance of Things Past,*
The great re-flowering of late summer surrounded us,
Coneflowers, queen anne's lace, teasle, goldenrod, clover,

As if chance sowed those flowerbeds, formal borders
Along the paths of happenstance and wild evanescence.
Today the wind is cold, shifting and reversing the leaves
To expose the pallid undersides like cirrus clouds, or
Tearing them, stormed from the branches like dappled snow.

# September

## But They Come Back Again

Over in the lower swathe of meadow
Hidden between cornfields and a row
Of wind-plied cherry trees,
The butterflies were thick a week ago.
Now only a soft luna moth or two
Lifts sideways on the breeze,

The colder breath of sunset. Slowly turning
Home I think I see a painted wing,
Which proves a sumac leaf.
Another bright illusion, holding on
Like traces of the children, orison
Or gold-framed photograph.

# Four from the Berggarten, Hannover

## Auracaria

How far north Hannover lies, not many miles withdrawn
From the cold Baltic Sea, its train of shadowy islands,
Open to the north wind that sweeps unanswered, unopposed
Down from the Luneberg Heath like a clan of brigands.

Yet in the Duke of Hannover's Mountain Garden,
Outside the close-built greenhouse, pane upon pane
Of sun-inducing glass, outside the walls that shine,
One Aracaria tree remains, despite its exile. Constant

Winter after winter, it holds its ground, flourishing
Sabre branches, parrying the wind's invisible swords,
Blown snow, icy rain, lightning, as if it still stood
Rooted, at home, on Patagonia's mild Pacific shore.


## Weeping Cedar

Stopping beside an oddly fashioned tree,
I check the label: it's a *Trauerzeder.*
Ah, I know that word:
A *Trauerspiel*'s a tragedy, where tears
Play wisdom's distillate.

If I were chased by immigrant Apollo,
I wouldn't change into a laurel tree,
But coax my calyx branches
Back down toward earth that raised me
Cedar or willow.

And if I wept a cup of tears, of leaves,
I wouldn't offer them
To thirstless deity,
Only to one who knows the taste of wisdom,
So salt and bitter.

Fagus Sylvatica Tortuosa

What makes that tree turn underground,
Burying its own branches like transversal roots,
Then forcing them back up, erupting
Twenty feet away as if a thick trajectory
Of dolphin, then back downward under-wave,
Back under moss and leaf mold. Oh, but where
It meets the light it twists: the lithe gray bole
Spirals upon itself and curves in air.

Witch trees, farmers in the hills baptized them,
Then driven by Pietism cut them down.
Beech tree, ironwood, weaving a snare of branches.
But step inside and feel your heart beat faster,
As if from fear or passion, as if you'd become
The heart itself trapped in its cage of bone.


Paradise

Almost October, and the sky still burnished
With summer, and the beds still overblown
With coneflowers, white daisies, black-eyed Susan,
And swales of goldenrod like heavy sunshine.

Paths that wind among the dark magnolias,
Rhododendrons, Japanese azaleas,
Define the boundaries of "Paradise,"
According to a pleated garden plan,

And lead to the Victorian Mausoleum
Where Hannover (duke, elector, king or queen)
Is laid in state behind cast iron doors
And heavier, three-story marble pillars.

So there we sat, with paradise before us,
And shadowy royal sepulchers behind,
Suspended in the eternity of bees,
The sweet inertial motion of our lives

Still undistinguished from the rest of love,
Until the stroke of midday with its chimed
Accelerations broke our reverie
And chased us from the garden into time.

## Elegy for the Tussey Ridge: Fracking Comes to Central Pennsylvania

*For Julia Spicher Kasdorf*

Those hills that bound the valley where I live
And breathe and walk within and have my being
As the old prayer book I grew up with claims
We stand related to the God in whom
The prayer book also chides us to believe....

Those hills, just where I gaze across the fields
Thinking how green they look in early fall,
Thinking how soon that fluid braid of red
And gold or violet will climb the slopes
A month from now, discouraging the verdure,
Making it shine, subduing its expanses,
Preparing us for the white cold that follows:
The sum of the whole spectrum is white light.

Those hills, I learn today, conceal two things:
A pipeline up the ridge at Pleasant Gap
Beside my favorite trail along a stream
Jungled by rhododendrons in the spring
That bloom like galaxies; and at its foot
A square compressor station. Who discerns
The stream of black threading the Tussey Ridge,
Ribbons of black entangled in a knot
That mocks the tangle of the human heart
Where all the colors concentrate and burn?

# Bittersweet

"I want the colors," Mary-Frances said,
Crossing blackberry whips to pull
An endless length of red and yellow berries,
"Red and yellow." Robbie told its name,
"That's bittersweet," without the irony
That pulled in me, an endless length, although
Benjamin silently heard it. And then "Stop,"
Said William, pointing to the autumn sun
Flush with the distant hill, whose changing sign
Halted our caravan: yellow to red.

## The Dream of Chaucer

Chaucer's *Parliament of Fowls* reveals
That poetry is part of the real world,
More like a metonym than metaphor.
The way that poetry acts within the world
(Given the sociability of language)
Helps us engender knowledge
And take the vows of marriage, thus: I do.
So in this poem, Chaucer quits the phantoms
That speculated in *The House of Fame*
But never passed the mirrored walls of selfhood.

Chaucer's speaker tells us that he reads
Incessantly, for pleasure and for learning,
For *lust and lore,* and oftenest of love,
*A certeyn thing to learn,*
Since both philosophers and lovers seek
An order of knowledge outside the observer.
The dream becomes a garden, nature governed,
And then the second government of speech.

Perhaps the secret of the writer's art
Also intensifies a lover's making.
Chaucer begins his poem with a proverb:
*The lyf so short, the craft so long to lerne,*
*Th'assay so hard, so sharp the conquerynge,*
*The dredful joye alwey that slit so yerne:*
*Al this I mene by Love. . . .*
As if the poet were a gardener
Pruning and grafting nature's plenitude.

The birds' debate and congress
Mixes up color, class, and temperament,
A loud uproarious turmoil Nature strives
To bring to order. All the lesser birds
Must wait until three proud male eagles sue
The *formel egle* for her hand; but she
Refuses to decide, which sparks a chaos
Of squawks from those whose pairings she delays.
Yet resolution triumphs,
And abstract principle is reconciled
With all the crazy, bright particulars.

*The House of Fame*'s a poem trapped inside
Bare subjectivity. As he matures,
Chaucer seeks rather for the *certeyn thing*
That in the *Parliament of Fowls* uncovers
A newfound realism: love and making
Are things intelligible in their own right
Apart from sense perception, wish, illusion.
What else is congress for? To forge a bond
Between the species and particulars;
To posit erotic governance
Tolerant of conflict and odd persons,
At home within the quarrelsome wide world.

Thus Chaucer as a storyteller learns
To relish the strangeness of his characters,
The distance of the past, the rich concreteness
Of moment, speech, locale.
So married people honor the loved other
Who can't be reinscribed in one's own soul.
*The lyf so short, the craft so long to lerne.*
And Chaucer finds himself at last prepared
To sit and write the *Canterbury Tales*.

## Roses

A glowing line, a rosy tautly drawn
And now unraveling, feathering streamline crossed
The lucent early morning blue of sky
Beyond high windows, here in the chateau.

It was a sign, and wasn't. Another line
Bisected it, another slowly traced
A parallel of lanes: flight patterns over Paris.
Everyone wants to come to earth at dawn.

Great events involve men on the move
With guns and tanks, explosions in the air
Falling to ground as stars, then cloudy ash,
Then chemicals that kill thirty years later.

When I first came to Paris, walls were often
Scored with bullet holes, as a reminder.
Now the walls are plastered or filled in
Or I forget to see what I remember.

Now that I'm getting old, I fail to see
Catastrophe as greatness. The bright lines
Lead to my rosebush on the windowsill,
Indoors not out, and lowly aerial.

The rosebush of the twentieth century,
Despite its charnel greatness, bore two flowers:
*One vote, one soul* and *school for every child,*
Honored often in absence, but still honored.

Praise the roses, tend the soil and water,
Vote twice yearly, raise your children well
So they can read the writing on the walls
And in the sky, before it fades and falls.

# The River Painter (1984)

# Gathering of Friends, after the Fall of the Sung Dynasty

*Bamboo, rock and tall pine, by Ni Tsan*

Four friends got drunk together late one night.
The talk, the waning hours,
The cavernous yawn of the moon through the window,
The wine and the color of the wine
Intoxicated and ignited them.
To mark their celebration
The host unfurled a roll of silk:
One by one they took the brush,
Mixed up the ink, and wrote
What their hearts bid them write.

The first one's slurred but graceful hand
Set a tree ingrown like a will denied,
Fisting itself against the wind;
Then added four dark lines of characters,
Crows in the sky calling their names:
We are the unvanquished black-haired race.

The next added a shadow of bamboo,
That wind lays flat against the ground
Until it blows itself to breathlessness:
Straightway the muddy leaf
Stands up again to flourish at the sun.

The third put up a drunken line,
A staggering array whose sense
And flow described the party's history:
How they were all consoled, then overjoyed,
Then overflowing, so they had to let
Their feelings take expression in the brush.

The last one placed a rock
In the low corner of the page
To hold the painting down to earth,
To fortitude, for all its play.

His conclusion in the end was just:
Their play came to its point
In the substantial courage of the flesh.
They were a soldiery of ink and brush.
I say that every man is equally brave
Who can confess he loves his friends,
Gives himself up to love of wine,
Draws out the secrets of his heart
And hangs them up in black and white. . . .

Especially when outside the wing of night
Engulfs the moon; bad fortune everywhere
Plays with the bones of men; unearthly war
Casts his red eye and brandishes his sword.

# On an Album Leaf by Ma Yuan

Two sparrows in their plume
Composed like folds of silk
Ride on the quiet brim
Of a long leafless waterfall,
Branches of the willow tree.

A sage wrapped in his winter cloak
Approaches through the snow,
Thinking perhaps of other snows
In threescore years and ten,
Of cherry blossoms, the long passage down.

His feet upon the frozen bloom
Make not sufficient sound
To rouse the sparrow or its mate:
But once he comes to stand
Beneath the willow, gazing at the sky,
He meets the sparrow's eye.

The silken eyebeam twists,
Draws thin, and breaks. The pair
Desert their dry cascades
For the securer sky,
Achieving easily the tiered
Pavilions of the air.

# The River Painter

*A Scroll by Chao Meng-Fu*

In the winter, after the New Year,
Chao Meng-Fu paints the river
To recollect himself.
The long line of the river bank,
The pale of snow or distance in between,
Mark out his journeying
From one year to the next.
He tries to call back who he was
At the last stopping place,
What face he discerned in the water;
His eyes change color
From blue to gray to green....

Once, gazing, he lost his visions
In the jaws of an ancient fish.
"Fish! Myself! I must recover...."
The old fish only laughed
And plunged back, its eyes tarnishing,
Into the mud of the river bottom.
Chao Meng-Fu painted that river scene
Again and again, the circles on its stream
And the fish at its heart, invisible.

But in the spring he lifts his brush
Only to give himself away,
To lose himself, betray and fly.
For spring is not the time to save,
But time to sow seeds up and down
The river's edge, leaving oneself
In cloudy paper skins always behind.

It is the time to venture forth,
When earth itself is scattering
Its seeds and wings, is letting
Blood into the swelling tips of trees,
The buds that fill and rise
To touch the inner chambers of the sky:
Scarlet, hot to the touch, about to bloom.

Then Chao Meng-Fu is master of his brush.
Placing it, just once, from here to there,
His in his godlike gesture re-creates,
Creates for the first time the river bank.
He becomes, like a god, at one
With his desire, and the line,
Like the trace of a god,
Is only himself, thrown off
With a god's abandon.

That painter lives his vocation better than I.
He throws off silk skins like his art
With easy grace, and travels by his brush.
He carries out his journeys on the silk,
By the true shape of trees, black rock by rock,
As I set out in word by word
Mere promises to take myself away.

He makes the stream unfold
Just as a reader's fingers turn the scroll,
Making the landscape open, the river flow,
The small boat drift on the waves;
And the dream of spring come home
Straight to the heart: blue river scents,
The sirens of the flowers, the irises,
Light flowering among the young bamboo. . . .

Chao Meng-Fu writes out his art
In black and white, with ink and brush,
In images as plain as characters;
His means are no more rich than mine.
And yet that puritan calligrapher
Can carry out the spring, himself ride
Transport of leaf and waves toward his desire,
Like a god in his image, divine
His own leave-taking, as at the scroll's end
In empty silk, the stream
Becomes the great dispersion of the sea.

# Belleville, Paris, France

*For Bruce Trinkley, who turns poems into songs*

## Dinner in the Courtyard

When summer tears the maple leaves
To lace, and blue shows through the green
Like those imagined distances
Weaving through all things close at hand,
Then sunset looms for hours upon
The scarlet tenements of day,
Unraveling curtains, windowpanes
Ablaze. The house is close, I say,

And more the table underneath
The arches of the maple tree.
Not even the curious neighbors know
If I am host or stranger here,
Nor if this roof of leaf and air,
The little courtyard of the world, is home.

## 97 rue Compans

"A spot of color!" said the white-haired
Gardener, her scarlet fingernails
Mauve with black dirt, her lipstick's red awry,
Tamping limp geraniums in a pot
Whose handles were the ingrown horns of satyrs.
I admired her industry,
But never was really sure about her motives.

Why did she dress so brilliantly to garden?
The courtyard throbbed a little in surprise
At its heart of darker green,
The barren lilac, maples and ropes of ivy,
Where spiders hung their threads in cotton foils

The landlord's son, who oversaw the courtyard
To work without abandoning idleness,
Appeared sometimes with a bottle of Ricard
And warmly encouraged Madame Labiche's progress
Among the potted flowers.
In fact, he seemed to have fallen in love with her
Despite the uneasy difference in their ages.
Though he never declared his affection,
He chopped off every lilac one day in April
And presented the lavish bouquet
To her confusion and everyone else's disgust.

Some people quickly forgave him,
Discounting his reckless act as a crime of passion.
But whenever I saw him taunt his timid wife
Or send his children out to buy him liquor,
I found it hard to suppose
His romantic, because impossible, heart's desire
Excused his various flurries of unkindness.
Besides, he often forgot or misplaced our letters
(Madame Labiche's he opened), poisoned cats
Instead of the swarming mice,
And persecuted the roots of the maple tree
Which rose beneath our feet like a buried star.

## Souvenir

I keep returning to the days I spent
On the other side, behind the Buttes Chaumont,
To half-remembered, ordinary things.

Shopping along the rue des Pyrénées
For tiny shrimp, translucent coral and gray,
Bouquets of aerial pinks
I carried like a cloud, glitter of petal
And violet shadow.

Under cover of evening
I quit my books and mounted boulevard
And alley to the courtyard—tired, breathless,
Pushing the heavy portal.

By the rue des Solitaires,
I keep returning to the same high ground
Above forgetfulness, above
The crowds of Paris.

I pushed the gate and always
Met the children spinning out their play
Around the tree of heaven,
Hesperus and Venus, as if the star
Of evening ran beside the star of love.

And you stood in the doorway
Framed with ivy vines, the scent of olive
And garlic on your hands. So I came in,
Smiling, hungry, bearing my gift of wine.

## In the Garden

> *"But where, where are the children?"*
> —*Colette's mother in the memoir,* Sido

Up in the hazel bush that stood for a tree
At the southmost wall of the garden,
The children lived like swallows
While their father and I cut grass
Underneath, and weeded and watered the yellow roses.

They climbed by swinging up on pliant limbs
And imagined a different home,
Disposing all they owned on pieces of string
Hung from the branches around them:
Dolls, bells, bags of raisins, water bottles.

Parts of the house became a constellation.
The children quarreled, sang and fell
On the hill of half-moon grass
We gathered underneath them, plash, unbroken
As falling stars against the roof at midnight.

They rose and fell, delighted,
Walked up the stairs of grass into their tower.
Although they never learned to fly,
They overarched the swallows easily
With their continuous invented music.

But where, where are the children?
I've been to the house and garden
Lately, alone; the bush has tassels,
The garden is overgrown, the swallows
Repeat their single note among the branches.

Perhaps the gypsies stole them.
Perhaps they've found another home.
Perhaps they'll come to light again next spring
When swallows travel back from Egypt,
Nesting in the ships that still have sails.


## The Last of the Courtyard

*For François Dimech*

Who will believe me later, when I say
We lived in a state of music? Passing birds
And mice met on the roof, and danced away.

Francis played his silver flute, and Guy
His violin; the children sang in words.
Who will believe me later, when I say

We lived on little else from day to day?
Life in the courtyard was its own reward.
Mice danced across the roof, and ran away.

Carpenter, painter, potter: poverty
Is the sole good a singing man affords,
Though not at last sufficient. As they say,

We lost the things for which we cannot pay:
Our houses were sold out, over our heads.
Even the dancing mice must go away,

Nothing remains of us but memory,
A fleeting minor air, absently heard.
Who will believe me later, when I say
The mice danced on the roof, and ran away?

# Greece

## On the Ferry, toward Patras

Corfu appears, and then the distant blue
Draws her away again: uncertain hours
As time begins to drown in voyaging.
No talk, no books, no breakfast taken late.
The sea, divided, falls behind the boat:
I see that blue laid back on darker blue
The way Odysseus must have, when his mind
Was emptied of its cleverness at last
By ten years' wandering. His thoughts are mine,
An island without houses, flocks or trees,
Undressed of all its causes. Memory
Slides by like waves against the running prow.

What memories could wake my tiredness?
The clothes upon my back, unspoken words
I always bear, or wounds from an embrace
Too often entered, now are all I own;
Along my flesh I feel them hardening,
A frieze that tells the future as the past
And scrolls my progress roundly on my breast.
I cannot keep my secrets to myself.
I am the figure of the ship, and where
I've traveled, where I go, what I will do,
Assail and tear aside the simple blue.

# Galerie Orphée

*(Olympia, Greece)*

*For Apostolos Kosmopoulos*

Now in Olympia wild carrot snows
The disenchanted temples.
Judas trees put on their scarlet flowers
And slowly let them go;
Tourists trample the dwarf irises.

But in the little hills
Where cypress form a balustrade
On stairs for no one, asphodel
Display their white existence undisturbed.

My friend, returning from his winter travel,
Opens his shop again for the new trade.
He carries marble children near the door
So they can see outside,
Removes a bronze Medusa to her corner,
Hangs the paintings in a row like windows

Slowly, with the same familiar gestures.
Through the painted windowpanes
I see him, but my voice has disappeared
Into another dialect of silence.

Truly, what could I say?
The endless contemplation of the past
Which travelers and lovers carry on,
Though natural, is idleness.

Not all our errant ways,
The skewed inertial line of history,
Can move beyond the compass of the flowers,
Nor slip from the embrace
Of Immortality, that bitter woman.


## In Medias Res

The whip of pleasure sends us all,
Our sensitivities bright red,
Delighted, lightly nipped, so some extreme.
Herodotus observed that at the edge
Of the recorded world, things grow more strange.
Hot spices and monstrosities
Are carried in by camel to the center,
Where civil, solid folk are pleased
To pay a lot for something from the corners.

Thus we who cannot travel very far
But in imagination, sometimes fall
Deeper into the boundaries
Than tourists like Herodotus, who saw,
Made notes, and came away
All the more Greek for what they thought they knew.

Hard at the center, we undo
The casks of Scythia and the serpent Nile,
Plunging through crimson, musk and wine
To find what we are dying to,
Our secret folded there amongst the spoils.

# Covering Ground: Bicycling, Running, Hiking

## Ruins at Jumièges

I cut across the curvings of the Seine,
Up the steep slopes a mile to level ground
Half-circled by the deep
White channel of the stream;
Though forest, fields and down
Again to meet the river! Cherry trees
On every hand covered their red in green,
While men on ladders pillaged at their hearts.
I left a trail of cherry seeds behind,
Though no one followed as I passed,
My bicycle as trackless as the wind.
So far from what I mourned, and should have feared,
I fled with more than Normandy in mind,
More than the river in my eye and heart.

An ancient abbey stands in Jumièges.
The western towers, twin battlements
Against the tides of darkness, still remain,
But every wall is gutted, overgrown,
And the high roof, the paradigm of heaven,
Is long since stormed away.
Between the nave and choir there is no stair,
No screen to keep the crowds from their desire.
Only a copper beech, the prince of trees,
Whose monumental bole could bear
The manifold thin nervures of the air,
Divides the floor. The leaves divide the sky
In panes of bronze that fan
About a spectral cross of red and green,

So the lost vault becomes a sheer
Translucent window, and the blue between
The blue of distance, as it ought to be.

I came to stand beneath the broken height,
And listened to the birds who did not sing
But flew like angels, portioning the sky
In principalities, dominions, thrones.
I mourned for what was lost,
Well lost, not knowing that my heaven
Was dust already, scattered at my back.
The wind grew stronger, scattering the wings.
I turned; my step was blind and halt;
The vaults above shifted and fell, a stone,
A leaf weighed on my thoughts. I should have known,
Passing through the low walls alone
From ruined paradise, not by the door,
The serpent at the heart of all
That love had offered me.
I walked out blind, not knowing where I was.
Not yet, not then. The light studded the trees,
But the great branching shadows, what I'd lost,
The evening tide, was all that I could see.


Marathon

*For John MacAloon*

Across the green that lifts and falls
Like ocean, like St. Mark's mosaic floor
Whose gilded earth the sea buckles and swells,
Turning on Venice that same supple force
She used to trouble other shores,
Her lion-headed ships her battering ram.

Across the green, how far the runner sails,
Spread out against the wind, his legs
Impelling earth until the earth recoils;
Or tacks without an effort through her hills
As easily a sailor on his girl
Sets out at night to bring his vessel home,
Slapped by the waves that rise and fall for him,
The lunar tide that sends him into port.

Perhaps he finds a current and gets on,
Arriving at Bermuda in an hour;
Perhaps a northerly and toothsome wind
Diverts his path, drives his tormented blood
To circle like a whirlpool in his heart;
He never has the leisure to prefer.

The voyage that he runs will never end
As long as time suspends him in the green:
His limbs fail, and are mended one by one;
His heart breaks and is filled again; his bones
Throw tendons, which like vines rewind
About their bole; his nerve fire off and on.

He always runs, through tearful hurricane
Or Indian calm; his steps are westerly;
The sea swells like an untimed heart, and he
Rocks like a little ocean in the sun.


## Spring Fever

At the wood's edge trillium shows
Mauve petals in three,
Blood-root fragile white
Planets down the ecliptic of the road.

I can do nothing better with my eyes
Than seek the early risers out;
My self rides up and down,
Teased from sterner purposes
By love and evolving spring.

Too restless to stay fixed
At my desk, which faces city streets
Through windows darkening
With dust and spiderwork,
I ride my bicycle by morning
Out to country at the city's edge.

I never touch the violets,
Quaker ladies massing in their dress
Of blue and white, the common pinks
Ignorant of their family's Latin title.
Empty-handed, given to pastoral,
By night I ride back to my lover's bed,
Trailing names of flowers from the woods.


## Edgewood Park

In Edgewood Park, the flowers bloom like souls
For Dante, haunting the swampy meadows where
I soaked my shoes, along the little river,
Under the bridge, beside the dusky woods.
The latest loosestrife withers, jewelweed
Shivers against the darker side of winter.
Sumac has turned scarlet, mint leaves bitter,
Queen Anne's lace to seed, carelessly scattered.

Autumn again. My dearest friends have scattered,
Seeds out of their houses, lovers flown
Southward to the heart's own Carolinas.
Things could be no different; such harsh changes
Had to be worked out to the last measure.
Summer's instrument is cast and broken,
My song spelled in dust, the empty flowers
Given wholly to their lineage.
The wings are long dispersed, the seeds are sown.
Close to the edge of my life's latter age,
I am surprised to find myself alone.


## Following the Dordogne

*For Sarah Glazer*

It is so long, Sarah, this time my hands
Wind and unwind, like the ribbon tangled
Inside my typewriter; when I try to straighten
The turned sentences, my fingers blacken.
One letter on another darkens the page.
How much better to trace out the curve
Of the Dordogne, as we did last summer,
Counting off roses from our bicycles
Along the river, pure
Because unnavigable.

Better to be laboring up the hills
That part the river valley from the uplands:
Wondering if heart or lungs
Would break at such crabbed epicycles, climbing
The highway tier by tier, until
We won the summit and the gentle grades
On the plateau, the bands of gravity broken.

The uplands were a different world,
Set off above the lush, close-cultivated
Patchwork of the valley, towns and gardens
Full of tobacco and roses, their golden smell
Of dust motes hovering in the afternoon,
Silenced against dank cliffs that held
The northern rain clouds like a cradle
Padded with moss, festoons of raindrop and fern.

The uplands were always spare, unwatered,
Fields not clearly divided by low stone walls,
Roadbed specked by rocks and the odd flower, pines
Turned back and inward by the unbounded wind.
The earth itself turned outward as it mounted,
The way a flower from its center opens,
So from our vantages we dreamed we saw
Across the hills' corolla the dim sea
A hundred miles down south,
The blue of distance swimming in our eyes.

Up there the sky was clear, as if the clouds
Had issued from the river, apparitions
Visible only in the underworld
Of the valley, narrow, fuming, blind with incense,
Where even the longest vision is constrained
Within a modest ambit,
So like the leap of heart within its prison.

Why sit still and wait until tomorrow,
Feeding sheets of paper onto a spindle,
Killing the beautiful whiteness with our labor?
How much better to leave nothing behind,
Practicing freedom, the river on one hand
And limestone cliffs made immaterial
By the gold leaf of sunset on the other.

I loved the way we traveled, fast and trackless,
Spinning mile upon mile
The great world's true appearance.


## Remembering the Ardèche

April plunges the classroom into light.
Aisles of elm trees glitter beyond the window,
And I must pause mid-sentence, wondering
Where you are. En route, no doubt,
Chasing the easy skirts of camomile
Along the Dordogne, south to Gascony,

While I remain suspended in my lecture,
Fistfuls of wit cast before flocks of students
Who long for the spring migrations,
Chafing at their confinement from the weather.
I wear my patience like a light green dress
And wear it thin.

                It must have been in April
You and I walked together all the way
From Langogne to Aubenas,
Never once meeting a window set in a wall
To sever inner from outer; only the high
Clerestory of sunny clouds raised upon hills.


## Ithaka I

Now it is one to me, and I don't mind
Letting myself fall open to become
Children, the vase of love, another essay
Toward philosophy unformalized,

Poems with no fixed habitat.
It doesn't matter, since the world
Resumes the place left empty,
Taking on the shape described
By nerves and girders, ribs and walls,
Collecting the light-worn substances
Our skeletons must somehow draw around.

I don't mind thinning into monotones
Of wind, an empty tree,
Flute bones of a bird that lost its way
In March, caught in the middle of its song,
A note, a rush, a nothing. The exchange
Is fair, the world allows
A hundred versions of equality.
Whatever source decants, the hollow
Conches of a fountain, wells again
With water, leaves, the passengers of April
Reinvested with their wings and song.

I don't mind filling out with memories
Of emptiness, a yellow sail
Once belled, collapsed and silent in the hull,
Or following the routes of pilgrimage
To marble ruins that refuse
Our praise and send us home again
To bury the white form of traveling
Beneath the kitchen door,
As if it were a hound that waited
Years for us, and died just at the hour
We recognized the sign
That says, no farther, here
Your dreams lie down.

# Science

## The Dissolution of the Rainbow

> *"By an extraordinary combination of circumstances, the theory of colors has been drawn into the province and before the tribunal of the mathematician, a tribunal to which it cannot be said to be amenable."*
>
> —*Goethe,* The Theory of Colors

A cut-glass chandelier dangled above
The desk where Newton read and wrote:
All morning spectral dragons fought,
Mocked him and made love
Across the white wall opposite,
Flashed their blue and sea-green scales, the fur
Of tiny fires, a glittering red eyelight.
Then one day they suddenly
Fled, and no longer were.

Rising in impatience, strangely lit
By reason, the philosopher undid
Prism by prism the trembling chandelier
To run her now constrained and broken
Offspring through a maze of barriers.
The light went through its paces
But the dragons disappeared.
What remained Sir Isaac quantified,
Teaching Nature not to sing
Her sweeter variations, but in one
Low tone, geometry, to answer him.

Although white light is manifold,
A mixture, so he found, of different rays,
Each ray could be identified
In essence with its angle of refraction:
This was the only origin of colors,
Color then reduced to numbering.
The dragons lapsed to silence, mortified,
Curled up and dry as worms a child
Might question in the fire
Of curiosity and leave behind.

When Newton set his prism work aside,
He wiped his hands, and wrote on creamy paper
Long and elegant formulae,
A shadow of the sensuous retained
In his illuminating study,
Even that much immaterial.
Yet he sometimes noticed, later on,
How his sines and cosines lay
Across the paper like dark skeletons
Of dragon, couchant, rampant as the full
Proud curve of the integral.


## Goethe in Verona

"I can't find it," he said to the almond-eyed woman,
And gave up his search for the day, rejoining her
On the highest terrace of the botanical gardens
Which overlook the river around Verona.
But I have every reason to think it's here
On the Alps' Italian side, where antique flora
Have always found protection from bitter weather.

He had been hunting that small, pale, almost leafless
*Urpflanz,* which is the childish grandfather of all
Nature's overabundant bouquet, if it exists.
It was, he imagined, a kind of decorous lily
Without lanceolate leaves or silver bells,
A true false Solomon's seal, that had no cause
Or wisdom to discriminate itself.

Goethe stood apart from his companion
And watched the tumbled red roofs of Verona
Changing to umber in the light's decline,
A little surprised at how his imagination
Failed him, since it had long become his custom
To find what he himself put into nature
Greeting their father like well-brought-up children.

The almond trees were just beginning to flower,
Spangles of blue in the twilight, fair and scarce
As Hesperus and the other early stars.
The earth was not yet green, but the voice
Of fountains sang in the last of winter's frost
And ten years' labor at Weimar. Little bats
Like drunken birds went sideways in the air.

He felt he could trust the circle of his five senses
As long as he continued to practice green,
Magenta, blue, and the complex strata of lines,
Designing the very life of Italian prospects,
As long as the little *Urpflanz* kept
Its peace somewhere, untroubled within a landscape
Waiting to be discovered, touched and seen.

What else could he feel, who suffered so profoundly
The music, scent and texture of coming spring,
The sheen of anemone and gentian, showing
Colors barely unfolded above the sheath
Of bract and leaf, like the Veronese lady composing
Herself at the edge of sky and marble plinth,
Her pearls the dimmer seconds of Hesperus?

Though Goethe knew very well that over the Alps
In Paris and London, the physicists of Europe
Were fabricating a novel ghostliness,
The truth of an underworld beyond the senses,
He still beheld the falling rose of day
Which drew itself across the terraced slopes
As the flower of light in blossom, not decay.


## Birds, Trees and Lovers

*Loren Eiseley,* The Immense Journey

Trees once suddenly learned the art
Of flowers, and inherited the earth,
We say, inventing time;
And birds have colonized the treetops
Ever since their silver scales
Divided, flared and lifted, mastering
Gravity, we say, keeping the books.

But neither the ornamental trees
Nor birds in the radiant sky
Oaring from island to island of brown
Blown crown of branches, take
Their place in our bookish time.
Perhaps because they are always perishing
Or because they live forever,
Paradigmatic crest and braided wreath.

Indeed, my love, since human lovers began
To read the clock or compass of the world,
Threading their way through the forest
Of symbols with clever hands,
We have liked to compare their splendid
Pleasure to bird and tree,
Reflecting on the solidly feathered diamonds
Perched in golden crowns above their heads.

"*Daimons,*" they say, "we seem to be
Always perishing and always perfected."
But they are deceived in their wishes,
Forgetting that human romance
Is a genre of history.
For when they walk out together, they never move
In a circle, but arrow hard
Through the tree's heart, and the house
Of the unschooled, musical birds.

# Germany

## The Poet and the Canal

*The Dortmund-Ems Canal, Muenster, Westphalia, Germany*

Canals run through a city
At a level deeper,
Straighter than the welter
Of superficial streets;
Carry out a slower,
Longer train of thought.
Daytime, full of barges
Trafficking like minutes,
Fleeting and as frequent;
Socialized by families
Of ducks and swans, who flaunt
Round their mechanical
Great cousins, brilliant
Steerages and rotaries.
Families of people,
Most often on Sundays,
Come out in demurer
Formations, but as colorful
And thick of plumage.
Banks stocked with fishers
Are richer in dreams
Than signs of fish;
The lines lead under
Uncircled surfaces
Sharp into fathoms
Of speculant green.
At night the canal is

Never so populous.
Waterfowl hide
And drowse at the edges;
The fishers have fled
To their upland houses.
Still, darkened barges
Are tied by the shore,
The stars in transit
Appear on the water,
Trees by the towpaths
Use the wind's voices
To speak to each other.
Then the canal's
Univocal flow
Is deeper and clearer
To late-night walkers
Who pause to hear.
Let poets recall
Canals to the busy
Forgetful city:
How through its surface
Of pain and confusion
That quiet channel
Runs like a vein.
Lively but orderly,
With some commercial
Uses, but better
Productive of dream.
Just a flight down,
Open to anyone
Who takes the stairs
Contrariwise.
That low domain
Our troubled higher one
Always sustains
And underlies.

## To Cathy Iino

I stopped in a forest
Of thin white birches
Today, at sunset.
Their silhouettes
Wore only foliage
Of flattened clouds,
Stamped with gold,
Lettered by branches.
Dear correspondent,
I wanted to send
So fine a message,
But it was hard
For me to decipher.
The silky light,
Or the characters
Both white and black,
Or the calligrapher's
Longing slant
Filled me with tears
Till would I or not
I couldn't see.
So I send this letter
Instead, to say
I wish you'd been there.
You who have clearer,
Intenser vision
Would know why I stared
And saw no farther;
Your absence stirred
And curbed my powers
Of transliteration.
So now I send

A different version,
Truer to loss
Than to satisfaction,
The longing slant
Blindly expressed
In character, hand,
Design and word.

# Letters from a Gardener

*(Michael Stone)*

## October 7

Do you wonder where I am? As the fates have it,
Those long-fingered weavers, I find myself
In the northern mountains of New Mexico.
Life suddenly came to an end in California,
At once too comfortable and dangerous,
Where lotus-eaters bloom on every corner.
Ten months ago I came to give a talk
On orchards to a group of farmers here,
And found the Bodhi needed a new gardener.
It's taken me ten months to turn my mind
From California, but finally here I am.

Six acres on Jemez Creek, which runs between
The constellated hot springs of the canyon;
At night in the autumn air, now growing colder,
I sit beneath that other milky way
Alone, in water hotter than my blood.
The place belonged before to Benedictines,
Buildings mostly low, built of adobe;
Large community kitchen, dining hall,
Rooms for meditation, pottery work shed,
Greenhouse, orchards, and outlying fields.
All day we hear the fluid sound of wind
Through the by now half-golden aspen trees,
And lighter music of running water, winding
Only a dozen yards from where I sleep.

What has always attracted me to Zen
Is just the practice of living here and now;
Desire for another, mystic world,
Desire itself, engenders suffering,
And the iron ego is its driving wheel.
We rise at 4:15 for chanting, tea,
Stretching, meditation, and then breakfast;
Zazen again, a little time to think;
Showers, hot springs, zazen, dinner, time
To be alone; zazen and tea; lights out
As the other lights come on in the cold evening.
Write when you can. Much love to you, amiga.

October 22

You see, the Bodhi's not a monastery,
Though we were lately visited by thirty
Japanese Rinzai monks, none of whom spoke
A word of English. They all carried cameras,
Shot rolls of film, and bought out every piece
Of the Bodhi's American Raku pottery.
They presented our Roshi with a bronze of Kannon,
A Bodhisattva; Roshi took them around
To Taos, Santa Fe and Colorado.

Sasaki Roshi, now almost seventy,
Came to America fifteen years ago
To teach, at the request of his own teacher.
He is a rock, whose center of gravity
Roots him to bedrock. He can see right through you.
Sanzen, the personal interview with Roshi,
Must be the hardest thing I've ever done.

The aspen and cottonwood are blazing yellow;
The Bodhi garden is still full of flowers:
Zinnia, cosmos, hollyhock, marigold.
And fruits: tomatoes, eggplants, carrot, onion,
Melons, cucumbers, squash (winter and summer),
And chili peppers, soon to be hung up
As brilliant sheaves of red, in front of houses,
Cabbages and Jerusalem artichokes.
Forty fruit trees in their second winter.
We're opening some untilled land to grow
Winter rye, first step in building soil;
The soil is mostly clay, redder than flesh.
Water comes from wells and irrigation.

I keep myself as open as I can,
Attend the discipline of concentration
Through faith that alters with despair, and hunger.
Already I've written too much; I just can't say
It all in so many words. You understand;
We suffer because of what we have forgotten.

November 23

West from my window virgin mesa rises
A half-mile over the narrow Jemez valley.
My favored haunts these days are Pueblo ruins
Rising eight thousand feet above sea level.
I sit and muse in the home of juniper, cholla,
Prickly pear cactus, ponderosa,
Piñon and all the varieties of oak.
The home of rabbit, squirrel, deer and elk,
Bear, rattler, coyote, and mountain lion
Visible sometimes at my eye's dark corner.

The sky is a deep blue, the winds are gusty,
Fast-traveling clouds will briefly mask the sun;
Warm days, cold nights, the coldest time of all
Is the still interval between dawn and sunrise.
Only the Russian olives across the river
Still hold their leaves; willow and elm stand naked;
Raccoon come down at sunset to watch and bathe,
To eat the harsh, hard fruit the ash lets fall.
The Bodhi garden's all but harvested;
Only daikon radish, turnip, kale,
Parsley, salsify, onions are in the ground.

I'm building compost, cleaning local corrals
And stables for manure, hauling in loads
Of leaves and wood chips from an abandoned sawmill;
Watching the fall-sown rye green the red soil
Ever so slowly, making a cover for winter;
Cleaning all the tools and machinery;
Making an inventory of bulbs and seeds.
The Jemez pueblo is holding all-day dances
For corn and harvest; we may trade some chickens
For Hopi corn, squash, melon, gourd and beans,
Chili pepper seed, and instructions for planting.

## December 6

These December mornings we are greeted
By the late-rising and last-quarter moon,
Walking across the dry grass to the Zendo
Where we drink green tea, chant from the Sutras.
How did I sleep through dawn so many years?
The lowered sun comes late into the canyon;
Morning work has already begun
When light slips down the steep walls of the mesa.

Incense of burning piñon drifts from town,
A smell which belongs in essence to the pueblos,
Especially now when winter lies on the land.

Weekends a caravan of pickups and trailers
Brings wood to town, some cut on designated
National Forest lands, and some just deadfall.
Most families here have summer gardens, fruit trees,
Chickens, and burn the gathered wood for heat;
But whereas once the houses were adobe,
Pumice, stone and wood, these days they're mostly
Prefab or mobile, foundations all uprooted.
The Atomic Laboratories pay good money,
And when folks go up now into the mountains
It's in an aluminum trailer, bought on credit.

The practice of clear-cutting lumber leads
To vicious erosion over the mesa slopes;
The fishy smell of money enterprise
Wafts up the valley too, developers,
Land brokers, marketing folly, greed and waste.
We already live so well, but it is never,
For our American green-stuffed lusts, enough.

Tomorrow is the eve of Buddha's enlightenment
Under the Bodhi tree, and so begins
A season of intensive meditation,
Daily sanzen with Roshi, and studied silence.
Here I stop writing, caught in the spirit of things,
And wish you happiness for Christmastide,
My traveling companion.
                              Siempre, Michael

# Letter from Germany

*For my mother, Frances Skerrett Grosholz, in memoriam*

Though it is only February, turned
Less than a week ago,
And the latitude is upward here
Of Newfoundland's north shore,
Mother, spring is out! It's almost hot,
Shimmering above and underground
And in my veins, where your blood also runs.
The hazels dangle down
Green flowery catkins, and the alders too,
Those bushy, water-loving trees,
Have a like ornament, in purple-red.
Spring is so forward here.
Snowbells swing in garden beds;
The pussy willows that you liked to bring
Inside, to force their silver fur,
Are open in the air;
Witch hazel in the formal park,
Still leafless, wears a ribbon-petaled bloom
Of yellow and pale orange.
Once or twice I've walked through clouds
Of insects by the river to the east
Of town; the ducks are back on the canal
Now that the ice is gone, loud and in love.
I wish that I could bring you here
To see this fast, unseasonable spring;
I wish that I could write a letter home.
But since a year has passed, you are
Not anywhere, not even underground,
So that the words I might have written down
I say aloud into the atmosphere
Of pollen and fresh clouds.
I say the litany of my desires,
And wonder, knowing better, if you hear
Through some light-rooted organ of the air.

## On the Loss of My Mother's Jewelry

One ring was sapphire, ocean
In a circle of foam,
Split diamonds. Another,
Two drops of blood
Rubies, a teardrop between.
As long as I knew my mother,
Feared her, loved her,
Her hands like emblems carried them.

Bracelets of solid gold, filigree
Of leaf and stem;
Necklace of little pearls, coiled gold;
Brooches, pins with butterflies:
Worn by her mother, grandmothers, aunts.
I have lost count
Of all that was lost,
The old trove she left me in trust.

The box is empty now, like a mouth in winter,
Not a pearl left, small as a seed,
No link of gold, gold dust, kernel of amber;
I have lost count
Of tears shed and wasted.
The line of inheritance severed,
I never will wear again
Those ornaments worn once on throat and hands
I loved, as I loved my own.

They are now laid by
In darkness that seals
Lost things away, which covers
My mother as well.

Her life's treasuries
Slipped from her early;
My loss is nothing to hers.
But where shall I lay it all up,
My corrupt treasure in heaven,
Now that the haven is plundered?

What have her hands, emptied twice over, left me?
Memories, grief, regret,
She left me enough:
My life in its prime,
Bright circle, with seeds
Of blood dark at the center,
Gold chains of tenderness, pain
Deep blue in the heart's mirrors.
Blind eyes, look here, I still wear them.

# Mortality

## Allhallows

I.
Flocks of birds along the Tussey Ridge
Fly south: as our desires are leaving us,
As ghosts descend and take their names along,
The very current of forgetfulness.

Instinct drives the birds; they won't get lost
Along the range of russet hills
That close us here, though some of them
Will never make this pilgrimage again,
Dropping from the air like rain
Changed into crystal, shattering
Their music on the granite shelves.

There are too many passengers
To name or number every one.
Surely a flight of chemicals
Arrayed around a racing heart
Has no use for a human name;
Why should we mourn for them, those bells
Chiming at the gates of speech?

II.
Leaving work at five, we go
Westward to the parking lot
Where our cars wait: perfect, cold.
Light flares and slowly dies;
The bars are gold, then iron.

As our desires abandon us
Like songbirds letting fall
Ribbon, apple leaves and bits of straw
Against the brown of autumn grass,
We watch them fly, half-blind,
Recalling still the under-scent
Of silky nape and tilted knee,
The nest of hand and thigh.

What we most fear to see,
A woman's body in the shadows,
Violated, faded,
Is just the small gray sheath
Of Philomela, feathers stiff
Around her bladed song.

Each gossamer that passes
Labors with a seed.
Beyond the veil of darkness,
Disembodied, brood:
Sing, tongueless nightingale.

## In the Light of October

*For my Aunt Dinny*

The long red seam across her throat
Shows where the thyroid, instrument
Of checks and balances within
The body's greater, delicate machine,
No longer lies. This afternoon,
The sleeve of light unraveling, she drank
A glass of radioactive iodine
To melt the last small edge
Of poisoned tissue down.

Now for a day she radiates
In isolation like a minor sun,
Closing the bedroom door to company;
And sits beside the window, looking down
On ranks of cattails autumn
Thinned and scoured, the Sound's
Blue mantle gently thrown
Around the shoulders of the cove.

Her husband, for so many hours
Unable to disturb her solitude,
Sleeps and wakes in the cold living room,
Imagining the rose
She plucked a week ago
From one late-blooming bush:
How radiant around a central gold
The shadows held like petals, luminous.

# Rodin to Rilke

That sensualist Rodin, who used his mouth
And nose to sculpt, as well as hand and eye,
(His models too, traced lovingly as his clay),
Said to the mystified young poet Rilke,
"Work! Keep working, industry's everything."
More in works that words, Rodin declared
That once he'd loved the easy, lyric line,
Nymphs flowing in a wave, or wings in air;
But now he took the harder, subterranean
Labor of making his way into the earth
Like a totem mole, a caveman, a digger of graves.

Trying to learn the paradigms of clay
He went for the gates of hell, not paradise:
Worked up a crone, dry sticks and withered breasts,
Balzac fat as a steer, the Baptist, blind
And blackened by desert sun, mad to the world.
It's the body, the clay that matters, and secret death
Like sex is the body's trophy. You have to get
Down in the cave to work out the springs of man.
"Black, damp clay is my master now," he said;
"You see how it stiffens, fires to a beautiful red."

## The Return

*For Pleas Geyer*

"Abraham makes two movements: he makes the infinite movement of resignation and gives up Isaac...; but in the next place, he makes the movement of faith every instant. This is his comfort, for he says: 'But yet this will not come to pass, or, if it does come to pass, then the Lord will give me a new Isaac....'"
—Soren Kierkegaard, Fear and Trembling

The gesture of resignation
As the Knight of Faith
Turns his hand like a calyx back
From the bloom on Isaac's cheek
Shows that no illusion blunts his pain:
Death lies on the rock.
Yet somehow Abraham regains
The life he laid aside: what floods
The empty circle of his arms?

The moon pulls back the waves
One by one from the sand,
Lace covers quickly, hopelessly unmade
To yield the empty bed
Of earth, the grave of love.
What radiance fills the place
From which the shining ocean fled?

The lover, lingering,
Turns down the twisted sheet,
The last silk leaves of clothing,
Hoping to see the other
Shiver, warm at the root,
The blood flow back like summer.

But in the darker wake of love
Each one restores the other, as they were:
Here is your own, like Eve's
Apple in hand. See, even the skin
Is intact, with its luster and veins.

So the poet to her inventions,
So the mother to her child:
Take, creature, your own true future,
Its shape no longer moans and hides
In me, but wakes in you. And when that one
Pulls on the globed
Mantle of its own intentions,
What does the sad creator welcome then,
What rushes into the hollow of the heart?

Blind Galileo, father of the moon,
Cheated of both telescope and eye,
What filled the dark horizons of your sight?
The dance of fire and stone
In order through the sky.

So the bereft, abandoned, blind,
Cry to their lost inheritors,
Go, you are not I.
The creatures flee and constitute the world;
The dance begins again,
The solid world, the moving world.
It is the world that enters in.

# Shores and Headlands (1988)

# The Gold Earrings

I thought that I would meet you here.
You stood on the pavilion beside *Nepenthe*
Where the view is still the same.
Nepenthe, you told me, means forgetfulness.
You reminded me to notice the body of earth
So often that our exchange
Melts back into a hundred other occasions.
Surely we admired the cliffs together
Descending and descending to the horizon
South of San Luis Obispo; singular pines;
The blue Pacific arrested in a motion
So vast and tranquil it resembles staying.
Forgetfulness pours through the enormous veins
That bind and furrow the world,
The ancient rivers of Acheron and Lethe.
Mother, souls who must begin again
Drink at those deep channels; so I began
Long ago the process of forgetting.
Not that memory grows less intense,
But the period of recollection lengthens.

I thought that I would meet you near
The lion-colored mountains,
Twisted cypresses weathered to silver
Unchanged by twenty years, the cyclic ocean
Enchanting and shaming thought into reflection.
Time came round full circle like the horizon
And placed us at the center
Talking together, drunk with the blue of distance,
Your voice clear as ever: pay attention
To the lovely body of earth. Nothing endures
In the end but the colored bones,

The mantling blood of ocean flowing down,
Forgetfulness. No less intense, I swear,
Just more infrequent as the years go by.

How body wears the mind in recollecting.
Tears blinded me at the door of *Souvenirs*
Where I chose a pair of long gold earrings
I loved and lost. The last I ever wore:
For later on my taste in ornament changed,
And they were peerless, after their own kind.

# The End of Summer

*For my brother Ted Grosholz*

On Narragansett's littoral,
My brother checks the damage, starts
To set his lightly painted mussels
Back to rights, around their bed
Of mud and grass. What animal
Walked over his experiments,
Blind to the order it unmade?

Creatures of the tidal zone
Are few, and manage their domain
As a refined cooperative:
So mussels make themselves at home
Most readily where grasses weave
Their archipelagos above
The variance of shore and sea.

"Federal funds, especially grants
Pertaining to environment,
Have presently become so scarce
We cannot offer at this time
The hope of a position here."
The sorry letters come as summer
And his research run to term.

He hears the deep disharmony
Of speechless voices in the waves,
Positioning his foot like Hermes
On the undistinguished mud,
Counts his creatures one by one,
Surprised how far his mollusks bear
Their standards, yellow, red and green.

Such rapid generations cross
His path, he wonders where a year
Will find him, why his father lost
The wish to live, and disappeared.
Those mussels are not stay-at-homes,
Sessile as barnacles, but spend
Much of their lifetime to explore.

Before they have become too great
With age, they often hoist their threads,
Anchor and mandarin whisker, pass
Like curious Magellans out
To sweeter, steadier terrain.
All this my brother verifies
In colorful geometry.

Dear spirit of inventiveness
And crossroads, parting of the ways,
If you can salvage your marine
A little from the muck of time,
Uncertain future, vanished past,
Then bring the gold proportion down
Upon that other life, your own.

# Nietzsche in the Box of Straws

What was real, in those days,
Except our endless questions?
Except the eternal return,
My love (who never knew
He was, all summer long),
So carefully expounded
On Saturday afternoons
To a group of curious students
In West Philadelphia, the year
I left, at seventeen,
My home in the green suburbs.
In front of my apartment
Crowned by ailanthus and dust,
A rosebush bloomed from June
To September; I go back
Sometimes, to see if the crimson
Roses are blooming still.
We broke for lunch at the Deli
Around the corner, that sold
Bagels and celery soda
We carried to the grounds
Of the Catholic Seminary's
Garden of rented plots.
Wild and civil flowers:
I'd stop by in the evenings,
Lovesick, exhausted from
Days at Horn & Hardart's
And the rigor of argument.
One day we canceled class
In favor of the zoo,
To see the hoary walrus
Snorting, heaved on its side,

An oracle, if only
We had the ears to hear.
"O thou dry-footed, ghostly
Children of the earth,
Regret your frail, ill-fitted
And so inflexible spines,
Learn from me the way
To be ponderous and fluid,
Like the visionary prose
Of Nietzsche, slipping under
The surface of the will's
Abyss, its spiraled blue."
All week I carried trays
Half-waiting, watching the door
For my dear philosopher.
Only the self-appointed
Connoisseur who haunted
The gold limestone museum
Came in for his cup of tea
Late in the afternoon,
Watching me bus dishes
Like an animate caryatid
Dressed in ivory nylon.
Only the Irish tyrant
Who bossed us around the floor
And flirted with James, the cook,
Who was easily half her age.
She watched us as we talked,
As I stood wrapping dozens
Of triples of cutlery
In napkins, trying to read
My ragged copy of Nietzsche
Stashed in a box of straws
At nose level. "Emily, what

Are you reading?" "Philosophy,
A German." "What does he say?"
"He says, we always come
Back to this very moment;
This moment will always happen
Again and again and again
As the universe combines
And recombines its atoms
In time's infinity."
"You believe that?" "If it means
We have to say to every
Passing moment, stay,
Be what you are, return,
I do. It's a discipline."
"I see," he said; and he did.
Only our regulars
Came through the revolving door,
Claimed their usual tables,
Unfolded the napkin, so,
Aligned the silverware
And nursed a cup of coffee
Until it was perfectly cold.
So the ingenious homeless
Domesticate the most
Improbable public spaces,
Between the fly-specked walls
And naked, faceless ceiling
Camouflaged by dangling
Lamellate metal squares
In multitudes like silent
Wind chimes, while the Muzak
Lulled us with its smooth
Reductions of Bach and Rodgers.
Only the lost and hungry.

My dear philosopher
Never appeared at my long
Imaginary summons,
But came at the appointed
Hour on the weekend.
So we talked in circles
Around the constant center
Of my recurrent dream:
He'd take me in his arms
And kiss me. Various, sweet,
Unphilosophical kisses.
Suspended in the moment,
I'd answer, if indeed
That moment questioned me,
I see that you must pass;
By all the crooked pathways
Skirting our finitude
That lead us out at last
Into the limitless,
I look for your return.

# Exchanges

*For Virginia McFarland, in memoriam*

"I almost found you a car," she said,
Driving me to the train in her husband's
Cadillac as sunset fired
Gunpowder clouds along Long Island Sound.

"My friend Dan died of emphysema.
I'd visit him in the hospital
Every couple of days and sometimes
Say, come on now, let me have the title.

"Face it, why do you want the car?
I have a friend who needs
That car a lot. But he refused,
Hoping, I guess, he'd get back on the road.

"All alone. He had no people.
I was the only one to visit him.
How did we meet?" She paused
As a stoplight melting into the red sunset.

"When I started to fish, no one
Would take a woman out in the boats.
I fished on the beach, loving to just
Stand thigh-deep in waves, to cast and cast.

"Still I wanted to try out deeper
Water, go after bigger fry.
Finally someone told me to ask
Dan, and he agreed, to my surprise.

"He looked after me, not letting
Any other fishermen
Swear or throw their weight around.
'Watch your mouth when there's a lady present!'

"He was really...." She made a gesture
Of something between ear and ear.
"Slow. He was. But also more
Careful than the rest of them, and kinder."

She threw one arm out in loving
Extravagance accompanied
By a ghost flourish of the plastic
Cigarette holder she'd given up for good.

"And he was a hell of a fisherman.
He thought like a fish. We'd putt
Through acres of indifferent water,
Suddenly he'd say 'Here!' and then, by God,

"I'd drop my line and pull them in.
He pretended he had money, though
Once when he was sick, I saw
How much: his bankroll scrunched inside a shoe.

"His landlady let me in to find
His mail. I gave him money then,
Out of my grocery budget, a hundred,
Two hundred maybe, enough to pay the rent.

"When he died, a niece suddenly
Materialized with regrets, and took
The little he left, including the car.
Then a lady called from Mamaroneck

"Who also wanted the car, claiming
He owed her: but she drew a blank.
He used to paint her houses. I think
She gave him money too, and wanted it back.

"In fact, the hospital official
Who took his case postmortem found
Social Security sent him nothing.
I have no idea what he lived on."

Sunset flagged and shivered in
The winter trees. She sighed, brushing
Imagined ashes from her coat.
"I don't like hospitals or visiting,

"But I liked him, so I went,
Watched my friend adrift in bed.
So after all, my dear, I didn't
Get your car, but you should know I tried."

# Vagabondage in Sonnets

## Saint-Germain, Paris, France

My bags are packed with magazines and scarves,
My cloudy head, my heart with memories
Bitter and dry as half-smoked cigarettes,
Flawless as a grocer's hill of peaches.
Finishing my coffee in an apartment
Close to the bridge that crosses to the Louvre,
I think of Delacroix's Algerian women,
Titian's Venus with her dark-eyed mirror.

Paris behind me, through the open window
Sunlight enters like the threat of love.
Occasional seagulls ride above the river,
Dreaming as I do of the North Atlantic,
Which I will shortly cross, bearing away,
Dear thief and lover, all that I can carry.

## Raschplatzhochstraße, Hannover, Germany

The passages of exile I have read,
Deciphering my own familiar hand,
Run like a major artery between
The heart of yet another radiant town
And the long corpus of strange neighborhoods.
Thus on a rainy summer night I stood
Suddenly motionless before a sign
That changed its green to red, its red to green.

I was afraid of the dark street, the gleam
Transforming on wet asphalt, and the sigh
Of planing cars with shrouded passengers.
Then it seemed possible to go back home.
How strangely hope allies itself with fear,
And crosses over to the other side.


## Mediterranean

*Near Marseilles, France*

"*Where is Ardiaeus the Great?*"—*Plato,* The Republic

Salt crystals in the hollows of limestone.
On a great, slanted rock I lay, like one
Of the sea's translucent children, caught
And finished by the rain of light.
So close the world's incurable inversion
I saw the thorny stars far underwater,
Anemone's dark rose the eye of Mars.

Wind from Africa tangling in the pines
Wailed through its house of permanent exile,
Who has brought us here? I threw my bottle
Of wine away, the sun drank me instead
As if I were forgetfulness. On the white verso
Of cliffs, broom scored the tyrant wind
Descending headlong like a soul in Plato.

## On the Untersberg, Salzburg, Austria

Another world, silent underneath the whine of wind,
The strange cries, like dry hinges, of the eagles,
Thousands of bees droning across rock gardens'
Embroidery on long grass, pasture after pasture,
Peak beyond peak: edelweiss, gentian, anemone
Weaving the summer habit of transhumance.
Shepherds lead their flocks up so many stairs
For these free riches, green to the line of snow.

Snow still rests in hollows like sheets of limestone,
But quicker, gone in a season, not an age;
Darker rock is studded with ammonite and coral
Left by a vanished ocean's vast reversal.
Silence gathers among the bonsai pines, knotted and corded
By wind. I hear the great stone ear curve toward me.

## Siesta

*Sphendouri, Aegina, Greece*

All afternoon the heat intensifies
In leaps, like goats climbing the terraced hills;
Another fig bursts on the tree; the olives
Surrender another cache of livid shadow.
Cicadas transpose their note to a higher key.
As if the ear were the most material sense,
They sing us back to flesh and bone, the steep
Rocky quarter acre where we happen to live.

But the eye is aethereal, that watches over
The tranquil cool Aegean, mantle of blue
Woven east and west with the stitch of wind.
We see beyond our country into another,
Familiar, never attained, where scattered islands
Gather like the dream's immortal children.


## The Old Fisherman

*François Dejanna, d. 1980, L'Anse d'Orso, Corsica*

He stands beside his ancient, lovely mistress
Dreaming of silver fishes caught in the nets,
Not of his dozen children, scattered to Calvi,
Ajaccio, who knows where; nor the somber Sunday
Visits his wife still pays him, bringing provisions
To go with the bouillabaisse he concocts with lemon
Or fennel and (always) a cork. He looks over his lines
Woven from rosy silk, like her body at dawn.

Nothing remains this morning of his old passion
But a brace of fishes thrashing on the sand.
The horizon is firmly drawn, like a refusal
To settle with human folly. Cupped in his hand,
She etches its palm with salt, alone among all
The forgotten, whose violence answered to his own.

# Letters from La Plata

## Letter from La Plata I

Blood sickens the air today.
It drifts from the pampas, from the cattle yards
Out of the past to contaminate the future.
I fear the present uncertain compromise
Of military and civil authority
Will soon reverse itself
To pour a scarlet pest on all our houses.
So from this heartless south,
This paradise demons have won and lost,
I send my love with only a few words.
Perhaps my solitude, the dislocation
Of Spanish into English, slow my voice.
Yet truly our conversation never ceases.
You are for me a diffuse and concrete presence
That circles in my blood,
Revives in each fresh impulse of my breath.
I sleep for only a few hours at night,
Teach all day and gather with my friends,
Discussing strategy till early morning.
My children wait to see me on the weekends.
I miss you. Patience, distance, stoicism
Are all I have to offer; my desire,
The shape of desire written on the air.

# Interval

> *"So are all Distances contracted in the Soul itself; and there Understood Indistantly...."*
> —Ralph Cudworth, The True Intellectual System of the Universe *(1678)*

I saw the love-light first kindle your eye
In *Pupille,* a little bar in Saxony.
Philosophers' congress. Cold November rain
Dissolved the window into constellations,
Flocks and spirals of reflected streetlight.
Two days you dazzled me, then disappeared
Like a star falling under the horizon.
Now at the center of the Southern Cross
You burn obscurely in my memory,
Dark retina that repossesses heaven.
So as the sky's imagined hemisphere
Is compassed by the pupil of the eye,
All distances contract within the soul
And there are understood indistantly.

Tonight again, a luminous cold rain.
There must be as much reality in the cause
As in the dear effects: so from your hand,
Covering page after page of blue, I read
The true determinations of your heart;
And this autumnal weather writes again
Your face across my eye's inverted glass.
We took each other with a sweet unreason
That crossed the boundaries of body and place.
For thought of a mile, of ten thousand miles,
Even the semi-diameter of earth,
Takes up no greater room within the soul
Than the short interval which parted us
That night, until you closed it with a kiss.

## Letter from La Plata II

A poet in this country can only describe
The drama of uncertainty and loss
In an orphaned idiom,
A broken language without history.
Who listens to my verses? My dead friends?
My girls, imprisoned, tortured, or in exile?
The past has slowly disappeared behind me.
Today I write to you while drinking maté,
A kind of Indian tea favored by those
Who are poor and mad. You see that I am both.
This government is like a drunk, vindictive
And unpredictable guardian
Who sets up the rules one day
In order to countermand them on the next,
So all its baffled children are bound to err.
The latest news is that the agency
For research refused my work on Galileo.
Four hundred years of conceptual advance
Mean nothing to those religious men, who find
In science only reason for suspicion.
(You notice, however, they don't mind buying arms,
The most contemptible and stupid offspring
Of Galileo's great intelligence.)
"Blind Galileo, father of the moon."
I like the way your poem honors the past,
Its bitter losses and his own
Long stubborn recollection of the truth.

# Exile

At the antipodes, where clouds of heron
Darken the waves and fish circle in air,
Where palm trees fall asleep, bury their branches
As if the heart of earth were another sun,
Our winter is your summer. So you leave
The city, traveling south over the pampas
To where the unquiet waters of La Plata
Melt into the sea's dark consolation.

Your small white house faces on the ocean.
Bougainvillea glitters on its walls,
Viridian spangles and a private fear
Staining your foreign journals, books and papers.
Perhaps the man next door, hired to survey
Your various pursuits, will be surprised.
"Tell me, Professor, yesterday afternoon,
Who was that woman standing in the doorway?"

Sunlight angles through the vivid leaves.
She waits beside you in her light green dress
As if a winter rose opened in summer,
*Dream of a shadow, creature of a day.*
You cannot see her. "No, I have no secrets,"
You answer. "Come and look. You were deceived
By the shadow of bougainvillea on the doorsill.
I live with that strange girl, my solitude."

## Letter from La Plata III

I enclose two leaves from my dear ginkgo,
Whose history is strange (as so, quite real).
Its parent tree arrived here from Japan
In 1882, an Emperor's gift
To celebrate the founding of La Plata,
And like a monument grows in the park
Around the corner from my parents' house.
In fact, many Japanese have settled here,
And one of them, a friend,
Promised me a bonsai from this ginkgo
Upon the occasion of our hundred years.
At first it was a flawless little tree,
Fragile and wise. But after a few seasons
I saw it grew too fast,
Excessively, becoming a kind of dwarf
Without a place in the great chain of being.
The more I watered it, the more it grew
Ambiguous and all out of proportion.
Today I think of us, and of my tree.
For we are neither the simple artifice
Of an affair, nor the natural expanse
Of love with room to breathe,
Foliage of such complexity and grace
It weaves a second sky. I mourn for us.

## Theories of Vision

I.
Train the eye to see
Colors long faded
From the marble throat
Of Immortality;
Colors past the sills
Of our red and purple,
Sheer embroidery
On petals of the white
Violet, white rose.

Train the hand to draw
Straight lines, circles
True as the simple
Motions of the planets
And elements that fall,
So the empty brush
Above white paper
Traces to their source
Rivers of the air.

The heart, impatient,
Tangled in her lines
Of stress, red traces
Of dead or living passion,
Must come to learn
With hand and eye
Certain renunciations:
The brush run dry,
Not sensual vision.

II.
Timid and fluid rainbows
Over the nacreous surfaces
Of shells, on peacock feathers
And soap-bubbles, appear
Whenever incident light
Reflects off nether and upper
Laminae of films, one wave train
Tagging after another
Like a younger sister.

Destructive interference!
Which, for a given thickness
Of film, only allows one color through.
So, on the peacock's wing,
Here it is royal purple,
There it is blue:
Quarrels of luminous children
Crossing, of space and time,
The unending recess.

III.
On the lawn of trampled strawberry and clover,
Your daughter blows across her plastic monocle
Sending down a shower of bright bubbles,
Rainbows clasping their selvages at every corner.

"Rise, oh, rise," she says, "fantastic creatures!"
Though even she must see the midsummer air
Is powerless to hold them, as the colors
Burst, all the invisible hands let go at once.

IV.
Visible light goes in
The eye's black iris
(flowering at the margin
Of a broad white river)
And never comes out again.
But absorbers are good emitters
And black is best,
So the eye also releases
(fresh circles on the river)
A different radiation
Invisible to itself, that runs beyond
The roots of crimson, darker
Than wine, or blood.

V.
Green leaves along the broken bough
Drink sunlight, breathe our element.
We lose each other every night
But dream of the recurrences
That unexpected morning brings.
There is no other way of having,
So the red-lipped branches sing,
And our waking answers them.

So the scarlet voices chorus
As the world begins to fall.
Every longer evening brings us
Home to supper by the fire
Where the last light, slowly breaking,
Fans its rainbow on the wall.

## Letter from La Plata IV

No, I can't meet you anywhere right now.
Be patient with me, dear, never forget me.
I need the warmth and solace of your letters,
But Argentina holds me here
Like a netted fish; my life is not my own.
You know I must still support
My parents, younger brother, and two children
On a salary inflation always reduces
To dust by the month's end.
Whenever I leave La Plata, my little girls
Ask the same question: When will you come home,
*Papito,* come to live with us forever?
And I stay on to teach philosophy
For my students, the young people, my own soul,
Although my work is dangerously wounded
Without the books I need.
Books! Those most desirable, necessary
Creatures of the spirit, form and substance
Of any innovation. They're never ordered;
Sometimes they simply vanish in the mail.
Be patient if you can, and more clairvoyant,
As I so often see you on the street,
The broken pavement by my parents' house,
In darkened restaurants and crowded busses.
This difficult circumstance
Allows no motive or strength for mere caprice.
I guard my love for you from hour to hour
Just as I watch my children while they sleep.

## The Carnival of Dreams

The ancient Greeks supposed
Blood the seat and transport of our thought.
And so it seems, for midnight
Brings you back embodied like a fever
Though you were driven from my waking hours.

Those letters ceased, that brought
Our endless talk across ten thousand miles,
The slow mail interjecting
Weeks between each question and response,
Time out of time. I guard the everyday,
Surrender to my dreams.

So early morning greets me in confusion.
I stumble to the kitchen with your face
Redoubling my vision,
Hands still warm and fashioned to your body.
Let my cup of coffee be the charm
That chases you back to another country.

The carnival of dreams suspends
Time in sweet illusory perfection,
Focusing our spirits till they burn
Like gunpowder roses, whiskey, memory,
Gold flowers in the blood.

However often you come back again
To that bright labyrinth of tents,
You'll find me there.
Embrace the girl you see
Three times: three times your open arms
Will close across the incandescent air.

## Two Variations on a Theme

> *"Fare thee well, oh honey, fare thee well."*
> —Dink's Blues, *as sung by Raun MacKinnon Burnham*

I.
Indian summer winds the trees
Without recovering their ancient green
Or leaving them in silence.
The enormous transience shimmers and burns,
Beating its empty vans on the dry hills,
An old song caught in its throat.

*One of these days, it won't be long.*
Believe the song, my love, and not the singer.
Wild grapevines string the lyre
Of branches, bittersweet half-opens, ivy
Glitters like the goddess's revenge
Snaking through the forest, killing the boles.

So weather sings, and flowers
Assume the claws of some fantastic creature.
Strange choirs out of season shake the air,
Rapt in transmutation. *Call my name.*
Apples ripen inward, yellow quinces
Bruise like mottled hearts, black walnuts
Tumble and litter the uncertain grass
That startles up, called by October's fictions.

Veronica follows the grass in all its errors
Repeating the savior's face,
Each leaf with its bloody forehead, lonely gaze.
*One of these days, it won't be long,*
*You call my name and I'll be gone.*
The body of earth continues to decline
Under the great, transparent shrouds of light.
Even gods are mortal. Trust the song.

II.
Light through the southern window throws
Shadows of cedar boughs
And the ghost of a jay, who haunts their frail
Shelter throughout the winter, on the wall.
Beyond the northern window, dusk
Stains the hills to damask, then to plum,
Sidelong to indigo. The leaves have fallen.
Sunset magnifies the neighbor's oak
To a system of borrowed light,
Thousands of theorems drawn
From the bole's exhaustive axiom: I am.

*If I had wings like Noah's dove,*
*I'd fly down the river to the man I love.*
But I stay here. Across the empty wall
Autumn displays its passages in shadow,
Recreating the ancient masque
Of emigrant light leading out all its flocks
Along the Susquehanna, south
To Chesapeake and the ocean. Daylight drains
Our darkened continent, and leaves a tree
Of silver rivers read by satellite
Whose eye revolves a thousand miles away.

Beyond the globe's meridian
Spring is beginning on the underside:
Tall grass fledges the pampas, passionflower
Stares from balconies toward Ipanema,
Ornament for the rich and shower
Of inaccurate gaiety over the favelas.
The principles of light reverse themselves.
I am, I see, but only insofar
As I have been deceived.
Ambiguous delight withdraws behind
The window screen, inflamed with visible night.

# Roman Elegies

*For Guillermo Ranea*

### Side-lit

Slow shadows cross the Piazza Navone
And sudden storms of pigeons
All flying left, or right,
As the grip of some obscure obsession takes them.
Who lives in the terraces overhead
Where nets of raffia weave through post and jasmine?
High-minded patricians, no doubt looking down
On swirls of us, importunate tourists
Bent to our cameras like divining rods
For ice cream, wallets, snapshots, cut-rate shoes.
So I drift through the lengthening afternoon
Thinking of musical D'Annunzio,
Whom Croce detested for his lack of rigor.
How can passion weave itself through long
Threads of analysis, the grid of meter?
Or how can it be uncoupled from obsession?
Passion turns one way, like Roman sunlight
Gilding the low clouds of umbrella pines.
So I turn left, and left again
Through side-lit labyrinths of streets
Between the Tiber and the beautiful shell,
Open to heaven, of the Pantheon.

## In the Abruzzi

Two hours out of Rome, Celano
Stands beside a vast invisible
Lake, which for millennia ferried
Sailboats and malaria.
A hundred years ago the new Italians
Drained it; now only an oval plain
Links the stranded villages
Submerged in melancholy and fertile soil.

Switchbacks wander up to the *Castello,*
Whose crenellations flank
A courtyard squared by the slow repetition
Of yellow Gothic arches,
Empty chambers fitted up with modern
Radiator shells and casement windows.
I perched in one to overlook the lake
And dream of the wrong man.

Give the grapes a chance to bloom,
So green and bitter still, despite the season;
Brush those wasps away from the ripe figs
They'd burrow in a day.
Let the cold wind quit the hills
And bring us summer fever unawares,
And send the stranger down. Or let him stay,
Tell me his name, he looks so damn familiar.

*Caro,* sunlight falters in the shadows
Of the unnatural palm trees that survive
Harsh Abruzzi winters.
In passes between Torre and Celano,
*Carissimo,* the snow will fly

Before October ends on the gray slopes
Above the ultimate pines, the bare unblessed
Walls of San Clemente Casauria.

Like one of D'Annunzio's abandoned women,
The cloister lies in skeins of travertine
And fragments of the rose;
Its vaults are empty, even the pigeons gone.
*Caro,* I think I see your face
In the squares of each provincial town.
This orphan passion fools me, since I never
Send it away, or offer it a home.


## The World as Will, Idea, *Grappa,* and Pigeons

Perhaps I've lost my sense of tragedy.
O pigeons who alight
One by one on the shrouded head of Bruno,
What have you known of life
In the Campo dei Fiori, these many years?
As I sit measuring my ounce of *grappa,*
I size up passing Romans in my glass
And laugh at the comic wars
Of love that stagger through my private opera.
The world has many crueler things to show.
Do I deserve a pigeon for a hat?
But every seventh man who passes by
Takes on the aspect of my lost
Beloved chiaroscuro,
Multiplied, refracted uselessly
In the dazzle of broken shade.
A refill in my hand, I say
Damn history's slow motion,

The tricks memory plays around my head.
Keep your distance, angels, curious pigeons,
I'm not a statue yet.


## Another Song

What do I want? A pair of espadrilles
That tie at the ankle; a kilo of white grapes;
A coffeepot that makes espresso upward;
A bunch of lilies (gold and adder's tongue);
A lady's slip of hand-embroidered linen
To wear as a summer dress
With ivory bangles and a double belt
Of Argentinean leather;
A studio with mirrors; a balcony
Hidden in oleander; a little car
Riding at anchor, tethered to a street lamp.

What do I want? Nothing I don't have:
An hour to watch the ceiling of the sky
Decorated by a hand
Intemporal, figureless, purely expressive;
A sense of the absurd; another song.

# Philosophy

## After *Timaeus*

*For Rémi Brague*

The serpent is all belly, and Timaeus'
Strange production nothing more at first
Than radiant limbs about a living sphere
Unconscious of itself, all eyes and ears,
Afloat in the matrix of the universe.

And what are we? Part snake, part crystal ball,
Our hollow belly the low sounding board
Where we first hear ourselves speaking or singing
And know we are the author of our song.

Sealed by the baleful birthmark of the navel,
We live with the necessity of evil
And breach our paradise, each time we fall
To speech, self-knowledge and the grand finale.


## Perceptual Acquaintance

*For John Yolton*

An oak that bears ten thousand leaves
Celebrates summer by my rented house;
Clouds cover and display the sun.
Objective but not formal presences
Enter directly the attentive mind.

They are in fact and always far away
As we walk underneath them, looking out
Into the cloud of green, the leaving mist,
Ten thousand swift appearances
That we, assembling, come to recognize.

They do not happen to us formally.
How could thought enclose a Japanese
Garden, woven cloud and bonsai oak,
Or open like the starry dome
With half of heaven really brought inside?

Neither in arrogance nor terror, turn
To the great external company
That we have never touched with hand or eye
And yet encompass with a fine
Awareness that allows its own awareness.

Distance is grace: whatever fell
Into the eye itself could not be seen.


## Letter from Durham

*To Ruth Geyer Shaw*

Dear Ruth,

      The lampshade latticed with amaryllis
You made from thread and parchment, reminiscence
Of a round that we once practiced climbing a mountain
And sing whenever our paths cross again,
Throws silhouettes of that twice-ghostly flower
Beyond its own perimeter and pole

Of glass jar filled with Carolina shells.
Life's small ironies. Your presence here
Haunts me in this uncluttered southern city
Where you computed flowers, started a family,
And left just months before I came myself.
The lamp lights up a corner of my life
On evenings when I return from watching stars
At their ordinary commerce through the coarse
Headlands and inlets of loblolly pines
Pitch-black against the paler stretch of sky.

Looking up encompasses vertigo.
Perception constructs its intricate rondeau
As it falls singing through those billion miles,
As light streams from the past, bending our wills
And eyebeams to self-limiting arabesques
Pascal commended and wise Leibniz sketched,
Summing infinities in their quadrature.
And yet containment yields before a stronger
Impulse to override all boundaries:
Our cosmos radiates, diversifies,
And where are we, at its expansive heart?
You and I three thousand miles apart
In the universal diastole must share
A collocation. Tell me where we are,
If you still guide me through the glassed-in green
Houses and labeled trails of local gardens.

Over the years, your offhand, patient lectures
Have made these zones of dark and light converters,
With and without the extravagance of spines,
Familiar country, closer, well-divined.
How you display the biography of boulders,
Tapping open archaic fruit whose weathered

Rind conceals morphosed or crystal flesh,
Two hundred million years of sleepy ripeness,
So old their age embarrasses the mind
With ancestors it shudders to comprehend.
How you lift up the glossy leaf of ginger
To show its homely brown bell slowly rung
By a fertilizing beetle drunk on pollen,
Or lead me to the early flowering jasmine,
Or summon Hesperus winking like a pendant
Along the ecliptic's true invisible chain.

Where are we, dear companion, looking down
At silent ancestral litter hung with garlands
Chlorophyll, water, and energy invent,
Looking up at stars equally ancient
Whose future we were, whose past we become.
Adrift in two infinities, at home
In the world intelligence and loving fashion.
Perception offers rocks and stars, red fictions
Shifting at the heart of constellations,
Runnels of iron staining the carmine-brown
Clay of the Carolinas. Inference
Offers us its embodied, sensuous
And therefore finite purchase on what always
Calls and eludes us: the wild boundlessness
Of Nature in her wrack of times and spaces.
Affection integrates the differences.

You stayed here seven years, and went away
Leaving the local pinewoods, gardens, sky
Full of proper names, gentle instructions.
I've looked for that low field on the edge of town
You sowed for the odd ends of experiment,
Counting its mint by thousands, measuring out

Their least parameters for the axial ribbons
A computer ties on clusters of information.
And though I haven't found your field of mint
Now surely run to seedy dissidence,
Their scientific title has a power
Charming enough to make this place familiar.
*Salvia lyrata,* like a spell,
Conjures specifically your musical
And saving grace. So in the end I truly
Find and miss you.
                              Love, from Emily

# Prothalamia

*For Robert Edwards*

## The Outer Banks

*North Carolina*

No ornaments but the double bed and open
Solitude found in older motels off-season
With solid walls and purely anonymous cells.
Our bed was like a boat drawn up from the gray
Atlantic combing beneath our balcony;
The sound of breakers interwove in the fine
Insistent pelt of rain that fell and fell
All weekend while we lingered, beached, protected,
Under the sheets folded like canvas sails.

Sometimes we followed the usual path of tourists,
Observing drifts of snow and Canada geese
Settle into or lift off grassy marshes
Through borrowed, diamonded binoculars
That brought them up so close they wavered on
Our eyes' own rushy edges, made precise
And flat by the forgetting of one dimension.
Flock in your eye, my love, whole colonies
Of gold sparks braving the darkened blue of iris.

We ran with our umbrellas pressed and flattened
Like backward feathers off the pervious wind.
Whenever the sun appeared at intervals
It scared up quarter rainbows in ones and pairs
Out of the low bushes like quattrocento
Angels. All things brushed against us then:
The braided strands, unbraided, of your hair
Glancing your lips and cheek, and of your hands,
The touch that everywhere surprised my own.

## Open Secrets

What can I tell of gratified desire,
The body's best kept secret? Open where
Passion divides our streams of consciousness
And love, inspired, stormy, uncommanded,
Seines the recursive tide.
Where you stand, naked as summer,
Half-absorbed in the conventional labor
Of rinsing coffee cups clear of their rimmed
Cream at midnight, while I rearrange
Mattress and sofa cushions on the floor
In imitation of the double bed
I lack. You are the heart of my invention.

Secrets of unexpected, slow transparence.
How love sets certain daily passages
Of fine print in italics,
Squares the odd capital in scrolling gold.
Beside your morning cup of Grand Souchong
Surpassed by a traveling light and quenched
By clouds of milk, your hands
Move thoughtfully about unconscious tasks.
I watch them lift the silver, ruffle a book
In search of fugitive pleasure, and recall
Their spelling of my soul
So many times embodied, here and here.

## The Ratio of Green

> "Among the colors, green, which consists in the most moderate action (which, by analogy, one can speak of as a ratio of 1 to 2), is like the octave among musical consonances or like bread among the food that one eats."
> —Descartes, Treatise of Man, trans. T.S. Hall

Among the colors, green, we are the sudden
Unexpected but undeniable
Razzle of new grass on the fairways, hidden
By a bristling copse of southern pine and maple
Behind our rented house. We lie protected
By so many velvet links from the emptying artery
Of dark red highway, bloodied with sheer speed.

Our green is sudden but slow, the unlikely
But inevitable offspring of long sleep, revival,
And then blind inches by inches spiraling
Through earth's brown leafy curls until the octave
Rings openly in air, so its vibration
Moves outward as impalpable spheres, as heavens
Raised above the players' lowered ken.

Still half-asleep they linger, listening,
As if they merely respected the ninety-degree rule
But, slipped from the embrace of that expanding
Music now translated higher, feel
Their loss as satisfaction with the green
Burgeoning underfoot, and walk away still
Slightly dizzy, ears ringing, looking down.

Then we get up together, conjuring loaves
Of bread for our breakfast table in plain air.
Analogy makes us the ratio of one
To two: two by virtue of separate stations,
One by virtue of music, a common color
Woven like memory through our conversation.
The clear relation of one to two is love.

## The Courtyard Revisited

Sometimes I only want to go underground,
Down my soul's obscurer steps, to the gate
Not guarded by Cerberus but by the minor
Bureaucrats of the Paris Métro, taking
The diagonal subway back in the direction
Mairie des Lilas, where I used to stay
In a courtyard now reduced to rubble, blocks
Of concrete haunted by ghosts of lilac and maple.

Not to meet old friends, love, but to find
You waiting in one of the possible small houses
And live there alone together for weeks on end
Unoccupied by any tasks but dreaming,
Reading and writing thoughts on scraps of paper,
Walking the streets in evening light that lingers
Till ten or eleven, running a few last errands
And then returning to cook our supper late.

Hidden away in that courtyard where no one comes
But memory, I want to lie down beside you
In a bed by an open window, listening
To swallows flying home as darkness falls
With the infinite slowness of northern summer evenings,
Holding your lovely body, tracing its curves
In the gathering blue obscurity and singing
Quietly songs known only to you and me.

## The Tempest

At last we climbed Michelangelo's Piazzale
To command the elaborate vista Arno divides
And bounds: *intaglio* of terra cotta
Or copper green pressed on the plains, and flanks
Of the tangent mountains.

Above us, not that cobalt Italian sky
Whose formal self-effacement frames and phrases,
But weltering clouds. It never rains in Florence
This time of year, but dictum's overwhelmed
By soft appearance.

Humid, warmed, the air grew up around us,
Thick citronelle of linden trees in bloom.
The perfume's German, and its arias
Of hushing leaves and muted summer thunder
Hauntingly northern.

Lost in one of those quarrels nobody wants
But history can generate as crossings
Of long entangled lifelines, we sat down
In the lee of a café terrace, half-protected,
Half-drenched by rain.

What else could we do but watch the tournaments
Of cloud? They wheeled on Brunelleschi's Dome
Fixed as invariant under transformation,
But meant to be seen against the wider flawless
Blue dome of sky.

For us its red tiles wavered, slowly fused
Like a stain on the winding currents of atmosphere.
The tears in things dissolve geometry.
So we observed by words, and the warming touch
Of lips and hands.

Daisies massed on the terrace drank the rain.
Later, an intermittent beam of sunlight
Broached the dusk, and moved along the hills,
Its path the fairest analogue we have
To a perfect line.

And yet how randomly the caressing light
Wandered across the quartered town and vineyards,
Planting its golden bloom on the linden trees,
Our café's raffia arbors, and the curve
Of the glinting river.

## The Cliffs at Praiano

Remembering backward, I foresaw you years
And years ago, in this lush obvious haven
For romantics, fishermen, homeless African wind.
West of Amalfi, east of Positano.
Our village curves to the sea in flights of stairs
Suspended above the beach a few small
Fishing boats, a clutch of swimmers, fill.
Whenever you enter our wide-angled, sultry
Hotel room perched on the cliffs, or call
My name from the balcony, your presence shimmers
Like a memory of great anticipation.

Every paradox religion loves
Seems true as the hour opens on itself
And we fall through, into that numberless
And unexampled matrix. As the light
Steps back across the cliffs, and one by one
Renounces the olive trees, the limestone
Shelves, the Saracen fortresses, the pines.
How else could God, uncertain at the cross
Of history, appear for us except
At a given hour, and how else could I touch
Our love except in these particulars?

We have been happy in a truck stop south
Of Roanoke, where shadows of semis loomed
Across the windows, browning the yellow neon.
Love can do without the props of romance.
And yet Praiano moves us with its wild
Theatrical display of elements:
Headlands, currents, breezes, strands of light.
Look at the cliffs, I say, and mean instead
That you are irrevocable. Reflected
Sea light gleams on cliffs day has abandoned,
Just as you stand before me, in my words.

Eden (1992)

# On Spadina Avenue

Driven by love and curiosity,
I entered the painted shops across Toronto's
Chinatown, and lingered
In one red pharmacy, where every label
Was printed in mysterious characters.
Beside myself, not knowing what I stopped for,
I read the scrolling dragons, roots and flowers
Intelligible as nature,
And quizzed the apothecary on her products.

Lovesick for my husband. She was puzzled,
For how could I explain
My private fevers to a perfect stranger?
I questioned her obliquely, hit-or-miss:
"Lady, what's this button full of powder?
What's this ointment in the scaly tube?
Who are these dry creatures in the basket
And how are they applied?"
The deer tails gleamed in fat, uneven rows,
Unrolled seahorses darkened on the shelves,
And other customers with clearer motives
Stepped in behind my back.

I couldn't say, his troublesome male beauty
Assails me sometimes, watching him at night
Next to the closet door
Half-dressed, or naked on the bed beside me.
An evening amorousness keeps me awake
For hours, brooding, even after love:
How fast in time we are,
How possibly my love could quit this world
And pull down half of heaven when he goes.

The patient Chinese lady, has no cure,
And serve her other customers in order.
Across the curled-up, quiet, ochre lizards,
Giant starfish, quince and ginger root,
She turns to look at me.
We both know I'm not ill with this or that,
But suffer from a permanent condition,
A murmur of the heart, the heart itself
Calling me out of dreams
To verify my warm, recurrent husband
Who turns and takes me in his arms again
And sleepily resumes his half of heaven.

# West Wind

I like to wake beside my husband's
Large resilient body, surfaces
My hand rehearses out of pure
And pleasurable habit, consciously,
Especially where his intersecting planes
Make saddle-passes in the uncertain
Alps of darkness pitched across our bed:
Where his neck and shoulders join,
His back shades into haunches, or his thigh
Looms into underbelly with a curve
Shaped by the most magnetic zone
My fingers graze, in passing for the moment.

I know each juncture by its hidden odor
Caught in the dark brown bear-fur of a blond
That sunlight easily spins to gold:
Basil, eucalyptus, harsh vanilla
Queen Anne's lace, cache of wisteria.
His sweet breath riffles on my cheek
As if day returning were the earth's
Lost children coming back again in April.
Who would wake from such a real
And ramifying dream? I switch the tongue
Of our alarming clock from lark
To nightingale, and wait with open eyes.

# Commuter Marriage

I.
Late February snow, and more to come.
No music in my bones, no bounce
In the soft elastic tissue of my heart.
The beat's uneven, pushing yesterday
Into tomorrow. Is this all I am?
A membrane flattening and rounding
Hooked to a calcium trellis
Blood and anima go rustling through.
One breath. Another breath. How many times?

Soul scrapes at contradiction
Like a bird against the window. Listen:
Thrill of brittle feathers on the glass,
Scratch of a leathery claw. O let me in,
Keeper of summer's house!
In to Tobago or the Carolinas
Where summer burns like driftwood, hot
On the horizontal coals
Under the delft-blue patterned tile of sky-wall.

I just don't want to hit the road again,
Driven by finitude from my dear husband,
Skirting the stricken hills
Where people seem to homestead in a daze
Half-unintentionally.
As if they settled there like snow
Beside the crooked road's decline
Midway between Altoona and St. Mary's,
Bradford and Kane.

II.
Wrapped in my solitude, I sleep
Across hundreds of miles,
And dream of my love on the highway
Driving to see me, driving away
Again in the chilly darkness.

He listens to news fade in and out
Of the small towns he passes,
Salamanca, Dubois, Bradford,
Each at the heart of a cloud
Of radio waves, invisible.

He hums off-key to the local classical
Stations that swell and falter,
Or a slow James Taylor ballad
On the popular bands he catches at last
In the ambit of Buffalo.

When he reaches the other side, he calls
And we try to touch by our voices
Over the crossing wires, the miles
Of folded and swirling air,
Of blooming and dry-stick meadows.

Nothing here repairs his absence,
Not his hovering voice, not even
His smile on the bedside photograph,
Not sunlight, clouds or hours.
So I must take my mending down

And stitch a stray thought to its end.
But underneath my breath I hum
One voice of a two-part round,
And sometimes in my dreams I sing
Both melodies out loud.

III.
Elm trees in the early close
Of winter take me by surprise
As dusk descends,
Take on, without my leave
Or wish, the color mauve.

A trick of atmosphere,
Earth breathing an upward cloud,
Or my imposed desire,
Or rising sap that swells
To leaf in winter buds?

Elm tree, shape of my desire,
What is color's origin?
Perhaps the sun's
Light reflex as it moves
Under the world again.

Midweek I live alone.
Desires rise and fade
With nowhere else to go.
Lengthening day, the empty vases
Fill and overflow.

IV.
Like characters in some fantastic opera,
We met in Pittsburgh, Boston, Binghamton,
My love and I, and Sundays sadly parted
At crossroads, bus stops, railway loggias,
In Newark's cloudpots, where the airplanes ply
Their version of migration,
Scheduled, unseasonal.

Long weekends, short ones, every parting paid
In the currency of patience and regret,
Midweeks *recitativo* building toward
The *arias* of Saturday and Sunday.
Mostly we drove, as if our cars were mobile
Musical anterooms
Between divided houses.

Morning light came up, or dusk was falling
As I'd pull in or out of that riverside
Unfashionable city with its bridges,
Olmsted parks, and monumental graveyards.
Verdi played in the background, and I wept
To Sills' high reinvention
Of Violetta's trials.

*Croce e delizia*. What mysterious power
Love has to drive us wandering over miles
Of dingy wilderness in search of home.
Papageno's right: the hell with drama
And squeezing life from monsters! What we want
Is wine with a square meal
And, close at hand, a spouse.

V.
Home. My eyes were full of tears
As I handed my obol to the ferryman,
My dollars to the woman at the tolls,
And took the last, familiar stretch of road.
There's the all-night donut stand, the endless
Chain link fence bounding the airport field,
There's my favorite beech tree. There at last
Our small green townhouse propped between its neighbors.
Oh, lighted windows, darkling silhouette
Where someone stands against them, waiting to hear
The crunch of gravel and the motor's hush.
So long, so far. I missed you very much.

# Waiting for News of Jackie's Firstborn

*For Jackie Dee King*

Your mother gave you a romantic name,
Dreams of erotic transport, opera lessons.
Mine named me for a beloved maiden aunt
And took me around to outlets for my dresses.
We loved our mothers, and we loved each other
Despite our mothers' mutual distrust:
Not enough stylish brio! Not enough
Tough intellectuality! They judged
Their daughters too, and so we judged ourselves.

And since we dreamed the ratio parent:child
In terms of mother:daughter, it now seems
Doubly riddling that you'll get a son,
As all the silvery sonograms foretell,
That I so far have only begotten lines
Of arguments and poems. Where's the girl
We thought would clarify our married lives
And long divisions? Somehow you and I
Must come to common fortune by ourselves.

# Elegy

*For Dana and Mary Gioia*

Dear Michael Jasper,
                         After a cold, wet April,
Spring has finally come to our piecemeal village
Stashed between highways, train tracks, airport fields.
Its boundaries are straight, but the vagrant stream
That puzzles local residents slips through town
In a series of crescents, falls and sliding fans.
So I take streamside walks, avoid the roads,
And think of you sometimes, meandering.

The season's rich, small boy: grape hyacinth
And lily of the valley burden the grass;
Musical aunts in the family of roses,
Apple and pear, play intricate variations
On amber and white, on cinnamon, honey, cream;
The maples cover themselves with coral flowers
And rush into leaf; the lilacs are almost ready
With clusters of folded incense, hearts for leaves.

Dear heart, green sprout, you'll miss this overripe
Extravagant wide spring, the very season
Most of us savor and visit in memory
To comfort the griefs of summer, winter's zero.
But all you know is autumn's fading gold.
Leaving us, you crossed the season's senses,
Sowing the fall with elements of spring
And now in seed-time, memories of snow.

# Pilgrims

La Coruña is a glazier's heaven,
Windowed balconies three stories high
On every housefront, winking at the sea.
We stroll between the ocean's broken mirrors
And their upright, Bauhausian reflection.

Considering the past.
Our past, so discontinuous, with midweek
Partings and reunions in the snow.
So many winter dawns you drove away
Dutifully, unwillingly, and I
Dried my tear and turned to the task at hand.

Each week we closed the difference, over miles
Of ice or snow or fog, whatever barred
The miles from Bethlehem to Salamanca,
Bellefonte, Tonawanda, Dubois, Boston.
The long, sad hills of northern Pennsylvania
And New York's southern tier,
Strangely reorganized by ancient names.

Each week you took me in your arms again;
We dreamed of Spanish castles.
Really, we dreamed of home. But here we are,
Pleased by La Coruña's glittering border,
Ready to complete our pilgrimage.

Galicia's green and oceanic hills
Roll up on Santiago de Compostela.
Our long midsummer traveling led us here
Because in separate, earlier lives we loved
The starred cathedrals, churches, shrines

That map the routes of Europe down to Rome,
Distant Jerusalem and Santiago.

The western portal quickens in the burnished
Guise of summer evening. Certain chapels
Are stained and dazed by mildew, the old plaster
Cracks in estuaries, patches of stone
Drop like small misfortunes.
But others are designed so ardently
In lunar Plateresque, sunburst Baroque,
That light is all we see,
And centuries of darkness fall behind.

Self-appointed pilgrims with their staves
And backpacks circle the plaza. Gypsy children
And hawkers chart their progress carefully,
Paying the purse seine out.
So deity long ago collected souls.

This place is not the same that welcomed pilgrims
Worldly and devout as Chaucer's kind,
And yet we too have come from far away.
Although we say no prayers,
We watch our votive candles till they fail.

And though we still have miles to go tomorrow,
And still no children and no common home,
Today we two accomplished one desire
That waited over years
While we, doubly and singly, bided time
And hoped. However often now our woven
Lives converge and separate, my love,
Today we've come this far.

# Revisiting Philadelphia

## Dark Tents and Fires

Narrow, encompassing, unsystematic,
Those late Victorian houses used to stand
Forever against my will.
Ten years ago I said: I want existence
Pure as Sartre's or Weil's, hardly a stick
Of furniture, and all the world in books.
I sank my souvenirs in hock or storage
And left the stubborn family walls behind.

Somehow the stones unraveled, over time.
So now my heart returns,
Wistful imagining at last embodied
In lamps and tables, dishes, embroidery,
The wrack of my old worlds in Philadelphia.
Worlds are manifold and have their seasons,
It seems, no less materially sketched out
Than Bedouin settlements. Dark tents and fires.

How rapidly my generations faded
And left their broken tapestries behind
For me to mend and set in different places,
Chairs to refinish, sofas to recover.
I fold the tablecloths and count the spoons,
Some of them missing. Where?
Lost in the trash, I fear, anonymously
Bent in evening news or toothed disposal.

Lost like my mother's letters, thrown away.
O save them! Battered eighteenth-century walls
And fieldstone houses, great white sycamores,
Row houses with their porches
Facing Delancey, Arch, Spring Garden Streets.
I count and count. The tablecloths are lace,
The napkins linen. Who will wash and press
These remnants, who will polish all the silver?

So many creatures withered from the source,
And only domestic ritual to guard them.
I raise my piecemeal household on the sand
Until another wave of emigration
Or dust or famine sends us all away
Or that day comes, named by a fatal number
Not infinite, but passing
My powers of inventory to command.

## Boundaries

Behind the hedge of privet, ten feet tall,
Was Italy, or all that I imagined:
A white Madonna on a pedestal,
Stained glass with olive trees curved in medallions;
And in the graveyard, families and angels
Carved in another tongue.
Capelli on the headstones, Serafino
Deep in a grove of new world cypresses.
Stone trees with their branches broken in mourning.
Gladiolas tied in grosgrain ribbon
For Domenic, Maria, *padre mio.*

On our side of the hedge, American
And measured off as neighboring backyards,
My friend Angelica Paoli
Showed me her matyr-cards,
Prayers embellished with a grisly death
On one side, flawless Easter on the other.
She told me there were statues in the church
Painted like life and magnified in gold,
Mary holding Jesus holding his heart
In offering to us.
To us? We never asked for such a token.

The lovely, canopied, unclimbable ash
In my backyard was like a pagan chapel;
Its crown made even Angelica fall silent.
But really, I was just an Episcopalian
Who prayed to God in church
Facing a hand-carved rood screen brought from England.
Really, I didn't know if I believed.
And when I left for Italy years later
I stayed so long, my father sold the garden
To nameless souls who tore the privet down,
Breaking our ancient right to boundaries.

# Sidonie

*Colette,* My Mother's House

Who's that in the garden? Halfway between
Exclusive nature and the world of words.
The garden is a garden because she said
It is, and made it so:
What grows inside its lawful boundaries
Is mostly what she thought to carry in,
*Rosier, laurier, sauge, ficelle de soie*
Up which the spiraled jut
Of blind, light-seeking tendrils take the air.

Except for weeds, and trees already there,
And stones the fertile earth
Keeps pushing toward the light, like frozen seeds.
She pries them up, expels them,
Or makes them orderly as walls and borders.
Revenants she never entertained
Come in by air or passing cat or simply
Pop up out of the ground
To change the garden's soft geometry.

Trace of a larger order:
The cat's paw printing a rose
On squares of chocolate drying in the shade.
Aphids in the copper iris, blackfly
Graying the lilacs, nettles by the hedges,
And fierce wisteria throttling the bower.
The tired, maternal gardener stands
And sighs, a trowel in one hand, and her silver
Scissors, dangling idly, in the other.

## Secret Places of Forrest Lane

Forsythia was a low arcade, a lair
Where tendril branches cast themselves aside
Over and over again, gold-studded flowers
In coppery green hair.
A useful place to hide
Whenever the fighting hit a certain pitch
Or simmered, tight or sober as my father.
My mother did what women usually do
Before they draw the line: dissemble, plead,
Scold and compensate and throw out bottles.
None of it helps. The drinker has to drown
In his own cups before he comes around,
If he wants to live enough. My father did.

After torrential snows
That flattened the forsythia and dogwood,
After the summer floods that made our lane
A small canal and killed the cellar pump,
After a string of blind catastrophes
That seemed like great adventure to a child
And trouble to my parents,
Inspired or terrified, my father quit.

When I crept out of hiding, there he was,
But half-transparent, like an earthly cloud
Gentle and self-occluding, self-enclosed,
But there. So my young parents ceased to fight
And picked up wiser habits,
Inventing my two brothers by surprise.
The township widened Forrest Lane so firmly
The border of forsythia disappeared.
I learned to live without it, now and then
Finding my heart a better place to hide.

# The Neolithic Revolution of 1956

Record snowstorms fell in March, and floods
In August turned the road into a river.
The age of painted cave and totem dream
For me was Forrest Lane
In nineteen-fifty three and four and five.
My family set up icons at the center,
Fixed among miracles of laundry, rites
Of open or slamming doors,
So many bottles, cigarettes and quarrels.

And fireflies and picnics and my lamb
Who every evening played the same old song
But truly, from the heart.
Beside my bed, the wallpaper was a garden
Covered in flowers with borders in between
I traced each night as paths,
Blazoned faintly by significant markings
Only I could see in the dim light
That drifted through my chamber from the hallway.

Reading put an end to those enchantments.
Sometimes at recess from my first grade labors,
I'd sneak back to the kindergarten room,
A bright, high-windowed space,
Open for nothing more than serious playing.
Papier-mâché and paints and clay and last year's
Giant Easter rabbit still in the corner,
And individual letters
That didn't have to bind themselves to words
But stood out all alone, like sounds or colors.

Life not yet arranged in rows of desks
Straight as furrows in a field, or streets
That governments can number serially,
Or pictograms in columns,
All the Neolithic late inventions
That help construct a world
Which afterward the clever, polyglot,
Manipulative inventor is bound to live in.
Run, Spot, run! He trails his inky paw prints
Across the page, and we,
Flush with our powers, chase him out of Eden,
Leaving the smoky mysteries and monsters,
The perfect flowers, impossibly behind.

# Legacies

*For Anna Skerrett Kirkpatrick, in memoriam*

Aunt Annie said, "When I turned seventeen,
Old enough to take the train alone,
I went back to Detroit, and the big house
My father had abandoned, where my mother
Anna Sanger died of scarlet fever
When she was only thirty, eight months pregnant,
Trying in vain to carry
His baby to term, and leaving three small children.
He shipped us to his mother in the East,
Locked the doors behind him, never returned.

"The house was sacked by loose acquaintances,
Renters, mice, and brave nocturnal children
Who spattered candle wax
On sills of jimmied windows, up the stairs.
All the satin drapes had long since rotted.
Nothing was left but sheet music and letters
(I took them home), the fruit-and-basket loveseat
That you and I refinished and revived,
Father's bookshelves with their leaded glass,
Handsome, but much too heavy to bring back.

"I searched the rooms for traces of my mother,
But found only those polished memories
I'd counted over and over every evening
When I was four, and suddenly far from home.
I know I have her laugh,
And probably her temper. When her brother
Came home to die years later, he bequeathed
Pawn tickets to us, and a fur he claimed
Was hers. Except the monogram was wrong,
And in its empty sleeves, the wrong perfume."

## A Poem for Polly

*For Polly Beardsley, in memoriam*

Hazel eyes, light voice, a stubborn jaw,
Honey-colored hair, quick moderate gestures,
The natural athlete's physical impatience:
Clearly, in my dream the friend I walked with
Arm-in-arm, was you. Still unconsoled,
You wanted a poem fit to settle questions
I knew I couldn't answer.
Who can explain the destiny of children
That hardens into drama as they grow?

Nothing occurs but detail.
We went to scouts and chorus and the movies,
Shaping the world by gossip, eating cookies
Equally shaped by our small reckless hands.
We babysat on weekends, stayed up late
And scared ourselves by watching *Twilight Zone,*
Or went to dancing classes
Decked out like little Madame Butterflies
And scared the boys with our intense illusions.

Sport was your talisman.
We joined the local swimming club; you headed
For varsity and won, and then went on
To pick up tennis too, hockey and soccer.
I think of you with something in your hand,
A ball, a towel, a racket, leaping up
Beautifully to connect trajectories,
At home in all the elements but fire.
I wonder if you made it through the fire,

The one that stokes the last sublunar sphere,
Or Dante's Purgatory. Where you are
Is hard to say, and yet hard not to say.
Dear pretty blonde, you learned so easily
The skills of those who dress themselves in white
For tea or tennis, your success obscured
How bitterly you aimed at some perfection
No one attains down here
Where all of us have freckles, flaws, and scars.

Gray hairs and wrinkles now, if you could see.
At seventeen, you gradually went mad,
Divided as two incommensurate girls:
The model Sunday schooler, and the bad one
Who ran away from home and smoked cigars
And dope and even, I think, put out for boys.
You had two different voices, and you wept
Only in Bad; in Good, your eyes were bright
And hopeless, like a doll's.

"She's such a doll." You were, close to the end,
Fragile and artificial, your hair dyed
Platinum to imitate pure blondness
Instead of the mixed-up brown and gold it was.
You left your friends behind, and ran around
In Main Line circles: snobs and featherdusters
Swallowed your parents' booze and canapés
And laughed at you behind your back. You knew.
I know you raised a cup for old acquaintance,
Your everyday lost life, but you were out
Too far, the tide was running, you were cold.

Three months of college must have left you tired
And wilder still. At Christmas I expected
Your call that never came. Instead you climbed
Out of your parents' house one frozen night
To watch the stars, or worse, up on the roof.
Beside yourself, you faltered where you stood
And then let go and slid the whole way down
And broke. Your adequate, ingenuous
Small frame dismissed itself
As perfect snowflakes smoothed it in the dark,
First melting and then resting, ice to ice.

# Life of a Salesman

*For my father, Edwin DeHaven Grosholz*

Behind the small, fixed windows of the album,
My father sits on sand, flowered with sea salt,
Nestling my younger brothers on his knees,
My mother beside him, me on another towel.

Or else he's smiling, lapped by shallow combers,
Holding the kids so only their toes get wet,
Free from booze and taxes, the city office,
His territory, miles of empty highway.

My husband, late addition to the family,
Points out a disproportion: that generic
Photo of my father on the beaches
Stands for a man with two weeks paid vacation.

I say to my brothers, look, you're all contented!
Both of you blue with cold in your ratty towels,
Thrilled with the wind, the escalating waves,
Our father watching the ocean rolls its sevens.

Most of the time, he's on the road again
Selling fancy letterhead, engravings
The businessmen he calls on can't be certain
They need, without his powers of persuasion.

He tries to tell them. Fifty weeks a year,
In rain and sun and snow, on secondary
Arteries crosshatching the back country
Of Pennsylvania, Maryland, West Virginia.

Alone at night in one more shabby diner,
His pale self in the speckled mirror-panels
Is like a stranger's. He coats his potatoes
And minute steak in catsup, for the color.

He wants a drink, but holds off for another
Day, another hour. The gray Atlantic
Shuffles invisibly. He orders coffee
And maybe calls his sponsor up, long distance.

Or calls my mother next, with lonely questions
She tries to answer, putting on my brothers
Who sneeze and whistle, practice words like "Daddy,"
That touch him at the end of the connection.

The dial tone doesn't sound at all like waves.
He might go to a movie, or a meeting:
There's always one around to fill the shady
Dangerous intervals of middle evening.

He likes the coffee's warmth, the sound of voices
Circling in on wisdom: know the difference.
Protect him, higher power, when he travels
His hundred miles tomorrow, rain or shine.

His death lies elsewhere, hidden in the future,
Far from his wife and children, far away
From cleanly riffled Jersey shores in summer,
The gray Atlantic playing out its hand.

# Revisiting Paris

## Symmetry

*For Yves and Lucie Vines Bonnefoy*

I've cleared myself a place at a wooden table
Crowded with books and papers,
Work suspended by my friend the poet
While he and his family summer in the Marches.
The library's quiet, backward-looking window
Gazes onto the rise of Butte Montmartre,
Now lined by sober grillwork
And framed by ancient, velvet, pale mauve curtains.
Facing me, a cupboard stacked with offprints
Written by my host tilts gently sideways.

But I'm uncertain, writing where I sit
And browsing carefully through all these books,
Searching for what? A poet and a woman,
I find my culture strange,
When overwhelmingly the musing agent
Turns out to be a man, and in the wings,
The muted, busy companion is a woman
Keeping the children quiet
Or bravely imitating a bowl of fruit.

I spent two hours this morning cleaning up.
Bonnard was already in his studio painting,
Morandi too (Giacometti was still asleep).
Marthe was doing the laundry, wondering
Perhaps if they'd ever marry.

Morandi's three devoted, charming sisters
Were bargaining at the market
Under the fair arcades of *Bologna Grassa*.
Alberto's girl had long since hit the streets;
His mother, in Switzerland, was weeding flowers.

Bonnard's nude are almost always Marthe,
But the plaques say only *Nue*,
A naked woman, a cloud, moving and silent.
Visitors will praise Morandi's sisters
For their table's vivacity,
Pleasing talk and raft of Egyptian spices,
But fail to recall their names.
And who could list the girls of Giacometti?
Certainly not his mother,
Also anonymous and caught like them
In the fine, distorted nets of his gray pencil.

The world of culture slants away from me.
I fit its shelves and don't. Whom should I speak for?
Those wives and maids and models
Used to speak for themselves sharply enough
In the case of an ailing child or a bony chicken
Or beauty's indecent tariff,
Although they are silent now,
And never devised a poem or drew a face.
They sang, or sketched a symmetry on paper
That someone used as tinder the next day.
So lately I suppose
I have to weave two lines in all I say:
Recorded tenor, evanescent alto;
Fixed trellis, quick and immemorial vine.

## 72 rue Lepic

Beyond the second-story balcony
Foursquare maples and the delicate locust
Already spend the first of yellow leaves.
Birds spiral down to splash
In the crusted saucepan doubling as a birdbath,
Or the newfangled sprinkler, when it's on
To keep the roses cool.
Pigeons especially make an amazing flap
In the treetops, heaven shivers, till they fall
Plop on the grass with boots and blunderbuss,
A storm of feather-feints that ends in silence.

In general, the quarter's rarely silent.
August workmen bang the walls below
And speculate on girls;
Telephones declare from other windows;
Garbage rattles down the flue provided;
And cars zoom up the street
Or break into alarms when trouble threatens
As it does almost daily, like the rain.

It trails the upward-puffing, earnest tourists
Searching for Sacré-Cœur by morning light,
And their evening counterparts
Hurrying toward the fleshpots of Pigalle.
They pause, discuss their maps, consult the sky,
And then go up or down.
But we stay in the middle, undistracted
By Perigordian domes or hot reviews,
Content with the reverie of painted wings
That plays to our borrowed garden,
And gold leaf scattered by an invisible hand
Trying to cover the debts of abandoned summer.

## Belleville Revisited

Enchantment passes, like an afternoon
Of sunshine that surprises us
Late in a day of cool and rainy weather.
It gleams on my old haunts, the hill of Belleville,
Sky high rises noosing the Places des Fêtes,
The curves of rue Compans, rue de la Mare,
Even the rue des Amandiers
That used to house the eighteenth century
Inside its little workshops, iterated
Courtyards carefully hidden from the street.

We walk together, watching the gutters stream
With briefly lighted refuse, useless silver.
So long ago. How often I returned there,
Pulled by love imagined, disappointed
Memory, and found and quit again
The life I borrowed sideways in those sorry
Neighborhoods. But now I close them down.

No reason anymore to climb
The rue des Solitaires, or circumscribe
The artificial heights of Buttes Chaumont
Where rocks are molded concrete, and the faint
Vanilla goddess in the air at dawn,
Wind shifting from a biscuit factory.

# A Son

## Listening

Words in my ear, and someone still unseen
Not yet quite viable, but quietly
Astir inside my body;

Not yet quite named, and yet
I weave a birthplace for him out of words.

Part of the world persists
Distinct from what we say, but part will stay
Only if we keep talking: only speech
Can re-create the gardens of the world.

Not the rose itself,
But the School of Night assembled at its side
Arguing, praising, whom we now recall.

A rose can sow its seed
Alone, but poets need their auditors
And mothers need their language for a cradle.

My son still on his stalk
Rides between the silence of the flowers
And conversation offered by his parents,
Wise and foolish talk, to draw him out.

## Thirty-Six Weeks

Ringed like a tree or planet, I've begun
To feel encompassing,
And so must seem to my inhabitant
Who wakes and sleeps in me, and has his being,
Who'd like to go out walking after supper
Although he never leaves the dining room,
Timid, insouciant, dancing on the ceiling.

I'm his roof, his walls, his musty cellar
Lined with untapped bottles of blue wine.
His beach, his seashell combers
Tuned to the minor tides of my placenta,
Wound in the single chamber of my whorl.
His park, a veiny meadow
Plumped and watered for his ruminations,
A friendly climate, sun and rain combined
In one warm season underneath my heart.

Beyond my infinite dark sphere of flesh
And fluid, he can hear two voices talking:
His mother's alto and his father's tenor
Aligned in conversation.
Two distant voices, singing beyond the pillars
Of his archaic Mediterranean,
Reminding him to dream
The emerald outness of a brave new world.

Sail, little craft, at your appointed hour,
Your head the prow, your lungs the sails
And engine, belly the seaworthy hold,
And see me face to face:
No world, no palace, no Egyptian goddess
Starred over heaven's poles,
Only your pale, impatient, opened mother
Reaching to touch you after the long wait.

Only one of two, beside your father,
Speaking a language soon to be your own.
And strangely, brightly clouding out behind us,
At last you'll recognize
The greater earth you used to take me for,
Ocean of air and orbit of the skies.

## Autumn Sonata

The ducks are raucous, flying overhead,
And all the talk you hear is running slower.
You don't quite get the words,

Not yet, but you can estimate the music.
Anger makes you weep, and a good laugh
Raises your toothless smile.

You stand to look, and listen as you sit
In the laps of people talking,
Wondering what the tides of life can carry.

Your hair is soft as milkweed;
Your father and I caress your head
Whenever we hold you, half unthinkingly,

And you move up against that stroking hand.
Your body curves along us when you're full
And arches when you're hungry.

We speak to you by name
And you look sideways, willing but mystified,
Trying hard to grasp at dancing straws,

To sing, to show, to answer, to remember
One by one the grape leaves as they tumble,
Somber oak and yellow jewelweed.

And yet for the most part you soon forget.
And yet I write this down
So you can tell us later what it means.

My voluble, mute son,
Who listen as the birds go storming south,
You know the melody, but not the words.

# Romance

*For Thinley Wangmo*

Bound to my computer downstairs, I hear
Strange music floating on another floor:
Himalayan folk songs, and the signature
Love plaint from the latest Hindi movie.
And in between, the baby's silver laughter.
When can I stop for lunch? Our habits change
With yak cheese in the kitchen.
Nor our lunch is rice with curried beans
And salty tea that tastes like chicken soup
Whipped to froth with a forked hazel wand.

Balancing rice on a spoon in the wrong hand,
I nurse the boy while Thinley tells us stories
Of life caught in the mountains.
Tales of ghosts and fairies, not inventions
But sober resurrection of her facts:
The child who talked to ravens, the shamaness
Who cures her clients with a bloodless dagger,
The wife whose passion burnt her to a leaf.

Even in this college town, she keeps
The shadowy romance of her native country
Double-woven through the warp of days.
Her husband serves the king by studying
Western administration; her confidante's
A wise collateral princess
Who gravely traded us a royal blue
Tibetan carpet for mere Yankee dollars.

Now it's where the baby likes to practice
His offices of hand and eye: he throws
His rattle down on webs of holy scarves
And swords out of their scabbards. Come and play!
Our son, it seems, is wise beyond his days;
He set our hearts on Thinley
When we went out to interview, and so
Brought magic to the house and the long shadow,
Jagged, fantastic, of the Himalayan rim,
And music falling like a mountain wind.

# Cassis

## The Outdoor Market at Cassis

Forty roses wrapped in cellophane,
Tied with purple ribbon. Goat cheese, speckled,
Redolent, moldy, squared in chestnut leaves.
Kalamata olives soaked in garlic.

Ivory gladiolas bound in sheaves.
Raspberries set like garnets, apricots
Displayed on grape leaves, golden *pommes reinettes*
Modestly wrapped, a blush on either cheek.

Thyme sprigs, lavender soap, dry artichoke flowers,
Statice, poppies, gypsies, children, dogs.
Wary Africans selling belts and statues;
Farmers watching over small potatoes.

Silvery sea-trout laid on marble slabs
Like miniature king salmon. Clicking crabs,
Dog-faced rascasse slapping out of breath.
Shining, trembling eels, short circuited.

## Excursion to the Third *Calanque*

The third and deepest fiord, furthest from town,
Has canyon walls that rise two hundred meters,
Raked white limestone pocketed with pine
And broom. So finely hidden,
So hard to reach on foot, the shallow beach

At the *calanque*'s sharp narrowing is silent.
No better place to slip
The summer population of Cassis:
Blare of cars and motorboats' excrescence
Vanish altogether into the hush
Of waves on sand. The ribbed, distended water
Is wholly clear, pushed clean by hidden springs.

We didn't walk in overland. I'm scared
Or careful about carrying the baby
On gravel-covered tracks that mount straight up,
Then tumble from pine to pine
Exuberant, crooked, headlong to the water.
We floated in by tourist motorboat,
The engines cut to a purr, the company quiet.
Our mate and captain dropped their explanations
And sat for a moment, watching:
Two old fishermen, tired of fighting the sea,
Yet somehow not content with their present catch
Of foreigners, Parisians, Marseillais.

Wind in the pines, waves on the lucid shore,
The fading archaic languages of earth.
Our translators knew enough
To keep it to themselves. The baby slept
With milk on his cheek, the run of his vocables
Doused in the fortunate rocking of the sea.
But once we entered open water again,
The mate observed, his wishes
Lingering on what we left behind,
"Can't stay too long in heaven." No, don't say it,
I thought, and the baby turned
Fretfully to my breast, and cried in his dream.

## Rain or Shine

The squall is over. Clouds have swept away
Their own long overtones and colors deepened
Across the seascape: purple, turquoise, plum-green, high above
Where the cliff rises, slanting rose and ochre.
The school for sailboats ventures out again,
A line of willful flower-sails that breaks
And wanders from instruction, reconvenes,
And puffs back into shore.

My pot of lavender on the balcony
Keeps blossoming, and rustles in the wind
That rises like a question afterward.
A weather helicopter skirts the Cape,
Transmitting part of the answer I can see
With my own eyes to all the inland watchers:
"Clouds drift down the coast
To Monaco. Dream of a cool but sunny weekend."

Shelley wouldn't have stayed here. It's too cold
And changeable for a delicate *souffrant*.
Whitecaps on the sea, the mistral blowing
Every other day, hardly a palm tree
Flourishing anywhere, except in hotel baskets.
Only a year ago
Winter frost brought down the eucalyptus
All over town, and left the apartment bald.

The baby's in a sweater, pants and socks,
Though he won't wear a hat. Half-potentate,
Half-prisoner, he went off in the stroller
Pushed by his musing father
Whose pockets are full of tax returns and letters home.
Our letters tend to ramble; we're getting tired,
A little, of our long term in paradise
Where no one speaks our language.

Don't want to live forever.
Don't want to climb the mountain, sail away
To Africa, fly high in a weather plane,
Hop a freight to Paris.
Just want to rock my baby on my knee,
Nurse him when he's hungry, wait and see
The shape of blue that opens up between two clouds:
The boy's light silver and his father's gold.

# Home

## The Pot of Basil

I stripped my office walls of travel posters,
Memorabilia, maps, the great charade
Of gateways to the world,
All the exotic places I'd rather be.
I threw out the Greek wine
Long turned to vinegar in its plastic bottle,
Lavender emollient, silk fisherman's line,
Invitations to openings in Florence.
The wishing-windows closed,
My office is only a cubicle full of books.

Nowhere I'd rather be than where I am
Now that my life has circled back again,
But home, a mile away
Where my small boy's just rounding the great Horn
Of dreams: da Gama, Byrd, Odysseus.
Waking up to the world at every moment,
He navigates the house from chair to chair
Ahead of us all and full of stratagems.

Benjamin, whenever I sit with you
Looking up and dancing on my knees,
Or sleeping on my shoulder, heart to heart,
Your steady breathing weight
Becomes the certain measure of my life,
Center round which the cracked sphere of stars
Can turn, as once earth's humbler citizens
Flocked about Orpheus.

With you fast in my arms,
I'm back again in the heart's Italy,
Safe on a terraced hillside facing east
Across the pensive Mediterranean.
Sailboats pause beyond us, close below
Fishermen gather nets on the shore to dry.
Oleander glitters in the hedges
And wind dispenses lavender and thyme,

Indefinitely. Content,
We gaze across the coruscating carpet
That stretches out to Poros and a pot
Of basil in the kitchen window, greening
In occasional winter sun.
My office shrinks and swells: it's time to go
Home to the little boy who waits for me.
How much distance does a life require?
Since you sailed in lately out of nowhere,
We trace our pleasures in a finer pattern
Of waking, eating, playing,
Pool and splash of sunbeams on the floor.

# Eden

In lurid cartoon colors, the big baby
Dinosaur steps backward under the shadow
Of an approaching tyrannosaurus rex.
"His mommy going to fix it," you remark,
Serenely anxious, hoping for the best.

After the big explosion, after the lights
Go down inside the house and up the street,
We rush outdoors to find a squirrel stopped
In straws of half-gnawed cable. I explain,
Trying to fit the facts, "The squirrel is dead."

No, you explain it otherwise to me.
"He's sleeping. And his mommy going to come."
Later, when the squirrel has been removed,
"His mommy fix him," you assert, insisting
On the right to know what you believe.

The world is truly full of fabulous
Great and curious small inhabitants,
And you're the freshly minted, unashamed
Adam in this garden. You preside,
Appreciate, and judge our proper names.

Like God, I brought you here.
Like God, I seem to be omnipotent,
Mostly helpful, sometimes angry as hell.
I fix whatever minor faults arise
With Band-Aids, batteries, masking tape, and pills.

But I am powerless, as you must know,
To chase the serpent sliding in the grass,
Or the tall angel with the flaming sword
Who scares you when he rises suddenly
Behind the gates of sunset.

## The Shape of Desire

Tracing an airplane's pale trajectory,
You always point, and finish, "Airplane *gone.*"
Waking from dreams about your babysitter's
Dark-eyed, clever daughter, you conclude,
"Lulu *gone,*" and hurry to the door's
Long windowpane to see her reappear
Freshly composed from memory and clouds.
Now you can say the shape of your desire.

Now you believe that each sidereal item
Carries a left-handed banner to describe
Through curl and dissipation how it was,
That every friend is summoned by a name,
Even in parting. You are wrong, and right
About the frail parabolas of love.

# Proportions of the Heart

*For Atsuko Hayakawa, Keiko Kondo, and Tadatoshi Akiba*

In classical flower arrangement,
Masako says, three major stems occur.
The *shin* stands thirty degrees from vertical.
The *soë*, forty-five degrees,
Is just three-quarters of the *shin* in height.
The *hikaë*, three-quarters of the *soë*,
Points outward, low, at seventy-five degrees:
Most often this one is a flower.

What a classicist I have become,
Impelled by the broad hand of revelation,
That is, by life itself.
Masako's creatures fill our country house
Like novel theorems from the *Elements:*
Out of fixed proportion, beauty rises
Unlike any that I used to summon
In rented rooms from floppy big bouquets.

A single sweep of branch, unflowering,
Another upward twist,
And there's the shape of nothing caught in air,
Somehow the proper counterpart of one
Or two explosive flowers.
Don't be afraid, she says, her fingers hidden
Inside the vase, to put more details in,
As long as they don't interrupt the lines.

The heart's most elegant, extravagant
Designs arise, I see,
From careful choice and rapid computation.
In half an afternoon, Masako fills
Our baskets large and small, and the clear vases.
Two leans from one, and three from one and two,
And suddenly altogether they compose
Their ratios to self-sufficiency.

Even the purple brambles from the field,
Cut by Masako, fall in whole ellipses,
And twigs repeat their angles on the branch.
So may you and I and our small flower
Flourish in the constraints
Space and number pose on families,
And make our tracery around the center
Of certain loss more beautiful, and sure.

The Abacus of Years (2002)

# The Abacus of Years

*For my mother-in-law, Mary Theresa Edwards*

The bathroom shone; the bath was filled with toys
That whirred and paddled for the babies' pleasure.
The soap displayed itself in shells and roses.

The mirror's sheen awaited its erasure
By minor orchids of a small, splayed hand,
The humid whole notes of an embouchure

Where one narcissus leans to kiss its second.
The rugs were freshly vacuumed, and the curtains
Beaten like gold to sift the dusty sundown.

Who was the agent, whose the strict conditions
That left the house perfected everywhere?
The children hushed their voices at the entrance.

Flowers on the table, flowers on the ample bureau,
Linen plumped and crisp in the guest bedroom.
A great white Christmas tree beside the fire

Circled by costly presents, a queen's ransom.
Grandmothers the world over vex their children
By granting the least grandchild's fondest dream.

The pool was heated, all the palms bedizened
By strands of stars, the abacus of years
And light years, half-remembered, half-forgotten,

Counted and discounted, lost and near.
Dear Tess, how loyally the house still welcomes
Travelers weighed down with bags and worries,

Children, principles, opinions, programs.
We miss the one whose absence still restores
This ordered disarray of empty rooms.

Old age is spendthrift; youth must count its treasure.
We miss the lavish habits of repose
Amidst our loud, unruly sons and daughters.

# Anna

*My Grandmother Anna Jones Skerrett*

Huron's cold wind shudders in the trees
By Anna's grave, grandmother I never knew.
It rakes the narrows gliding back toward Erie
Where my grandfather piloted
His cabin cruiser through the bounding 'twenties.
Doted upon by the symphonic Joneses
Whose brilliant daughter he abruptly married,
Fathering three children far away
From Philadelphia's teapots and his mother,
He charted a new world
According to the stars of home and office
And the church his wife's grandfather built.

Cold wind. A world devoured
By wolf-tooth epidemics all at once:
His borrowed parents and his wife
Who took a fourth child with her, underground.
Nothing left but three small children
He could only hurry to his mother,
And leave them all behind, abruptly.
Struck by cold wind down the Detroit River,
I wonder how he understood his life
When he ran off to Paris,
How often then he dreamed the revenant
Daughter of musical parents.

Anna Jones, red haired, hot tempered, fond
Of playing with her children in the nursery,
Singing songs my mother soon forgot.
Fond of taking the Athletic Club
By storm, invading the men's pool
With her three pretty ducklings,
Two splashing in her wake, one in her arms.
Fond of quoting Liszt on the piano.
Fond of my grandfather.
See, she hovers at his hotel window,
Encouraging a cold wind in the trees
Along the rue Domat, touching his cheek.

# Rondo, Andante

*For my Great Aunt Emily Paddock, my aunt Jane Skerrett Pierce, my grandmother Katherine Rolfe Grosholz and her mother Kate Da Costa De Haven*

The elements of light
That take the warm interior of my house
This autumn evening may be just the same
As those outside that hang,
Fading and brilliant, on the ecstatic branch.
Only the careful patterns of interference
That order them in air are various.
Crisscross bayberry lattice, rhododendron
Starred, right angles on the oak,
The tumbled arches of forsythia,
Piano music, Mozart simplified
So children may repeat him, and their mother
Who never played at all until this year.
Minor chords to fasten the filtered light
My great aunt Emily worked a century past
Onto her needlepoint. Relationship
Makes elements complex,
Therefore estranging them from what they were
As elements: so out of red and gold
A maple leaf arises, or a woman
Who notices how music has changed her hands.

And therefore harmonizing: on the stairs,
The children sit together, quiet for once,
Blond head, black curls in whispered consultation
Over a fleet of glossy miniature cars
Whose wheels will briefly track
The wooden floorboards and then disappear.
And on the table, alstroemeria
That lasts a week if anyone remembers

To change the water, statice, and yellow freesia,
And eucalyptus thrown in by the florist
For once for free, and indestructible fern.
Even the furniture repeats the patterns,
Each piece inhabited by a watchful spirit:
My luminous aunt, who tips the goose-neck rocker
That taps the edge of the 1940 hymnal,
Who might have rocked the ultimate foundations
Of the whole Episcopal Church, if she'd survived;
My grandmother, tilting the portraits out of plumb,
Who drove an hour in the teeth of a hurricane
Though she was nearly blind
To ransom them from my Grimm stepmother's house;

My mother, absently humming,
Who every evening matches up the bookends
That picture Chao Meng Fu's quite literal
Landscapes, each blue tree exemplifying
The character for "tree," and each green hill
The character for "hill." She once shellacked
Their ivoried surfaces in endless tedious
Sessions of *découpage* (her last distraction
Before the Master's and the botched divorce).
The quiet house occasionally filled
With Mozart, the inconsolable light of sunset
Streaming through locked windows.
And I'd stand all alone at the front door
Watching the maples flicker against the horizon,
Listening for train whistles, for the sound
Of diesel trucks roaring down Route 30,
Quite unaware the westward place I longed for
Was only my own house,
Its parts permuted and understood otherwise,
The way a mother begins to study Mozart,
A child's hand riding lightly upon her hand.

# Ben

## Where the Sky Used to Be

I.
Out in woods at night,
Looking up, you're so surprised
By two thousand visible stars
On blackness, you rub your eyes.
"Mama, we're in outer space."

Indeed we are,
Stuck here and rolling where?
Saved from daytime vertigo
Just barely by the false,
Sunny, dusty torsion of the air.

II.
"Hold me up higher," you say, then say louder.
I ratchet you up, and sigh. You smile
At your wish-granting mama,
Flutter your lashes. Promise me anything!
"I want to touch the sky."

And if I held you high above my shoulders,
Then could you touch? You get
The point, and wriggle down my arms, smiling
And piqued. "I know I couldn't." So?
The sky is our recurrent blue invention.

Seeing's social contract, all the shelter
We long for: ceiling, roof, beanstalk umbrella.
An artifact of wish. Country of air
To the unquestioning serious,
And to the joking questioner, not there.


## Through the Darkness Be Thou Near Me

Sometimes I sit beside you in the dark
As you push off toward sleep,
Your bed a boat descending ocean-ward
Along the Serpentine.

Torn by other tasks (the house undone,
The word unwritten), still I like that waiting
When everything falls quiet, even you,
Even my restlessness.

The whirr from your cylindrical machine
Supposed to purify the air
Of pollen, mold, and dust,
Leaves silence nonetheless impure.

Hidden, the pilot light
Beside the dial bathes half your room
In vague, unsettling green,
The radiance of nightmare.

But Lady Earth respires
Against her million pillows, and the pea
Of fire. Trees scrub the local atmosphere
Till midnight's sweet again. And you,

Tree flower, porous leaf,
Breathe lightly, stirred as if a wind
Were lifting all the edges of your dream,
And fall asleep.


## Real Bullets

Benjamin, son of the right hand,
Goes everywhere lately fabulously armed
With silver F-4 bombers, Messerschmitts,
Empty .38's and plastic rifles
Loaded with spongy projectiles that still hurt.

His thirst for battle lore is a tin cup
Whose bottom drains the Marianas Trench
And salty gallons of enemy engagements,
Air corps daring over German cities,
Fleets of destroyers carving the Pacific,

Flow in every day at breakfast, lunch,
And dinner from his well-instructed father,
Child himself of a Navy career man
Who used to leave his children six months yearly
To sweep the minefields of a finished war.

"Why didn't Dad grow up and join the Navy
Like Grandpa?" Benjamin examines me
Somehow embarrassed. "Ben, in fact your father
Tried hard not to get drafted. He never wanted
To land in Vietnam, sunk in a bad war."

"What's 'drafted'?" "Usually governments in wartime
Exercise their right to make citizens
Fight as soldiers. Male citizens," I add,
Turning to face my little boy, uncertain
Whether he understands. He understands.

"What?" he demands, suddenly agitated.
"You mean our government could make me fight?
You mean they could send me out on a battlefield
to get shot? Send me out in the open where enemy
Guns would really be shooting at me? Real bullets?"

The Messerschmitt nosedives to the kitchen floor,
And Benjamin, son of the right hand,
Is weeping, hard. And I, who equally suddenly
Understand the old doom of bearing sons,
Weep with him, and we fall in each other's arms.

# The Great Blizzard

*For Elhanan Yakira*

Snow on the Mount of Olives
Where stranded camels, brought in from the desert
Near Jordan to sit down beside the tourists,
Shudder and breathe a cloud;
Where tourists strain to see Jerusalem
Behind the snow: ramparts of the Old City,
Gold Dome of the Rock, vivid and faded.
Snow on the Garden of Gethsemane,
On massive, fragile olive trees
That heard perhaps a god plunged in a body
Asking the enigmatic cloud
For guidance, and its answer.

Snow on the gilt, ramshackle
Church of the Holy Sepulcher, disputed
Patchwork of black-robed, small sectarians
Staking chapels out with prayers and incense:
Clouds in the cupola, clouds in the gilded caves,
Holy confusion filling Golgotha
Where the dying god still weeps, petitioning
A silent patriarch, still bleeds and breathes.
Snow on the young Israeli soldiers
Shouldering loaded Uzis. Snow
On the Palestinian boys igniting threads
Of gunpowder on the sidewalk.

Snow on the tourists, scared, cold, and confused
In the labyrinth of streets.
Snow on the delicate acacias, on the palms,
Stripping branches in the well-built gardens
Around the pale gold, cubic limestone buildings
That climb the steep hills of Jerusalem.
Snow on the valley of Hell.
Snow on the Holy Mount where Abraham
Raised his knife against Isaac, under the sign
Of the patriarch, and where Mohammed,
Dressed for holy war with sword and steed,
Escaped to heaven.

Snow on the Arab coffee shops Israelis
No longer patronize, on modish plazas
Where rich and poor are not Palestinian.
Snow on half-deserted neighborhoods
Where boarded storefront, disembodied window
Spell out divided zones.
Snow on Fatima, snow on Ruth and Naomi,
Snow on the Virgin Mary,
Snow on the pregnant peasant girl
Still looking for her husband everywhere
Hopelessly in earth and heaven, who sighs
And weeps and walks back into the house of snow.

# Revisiting the Church of the Holy Sepulcher

*For Israel Charny*

The first time, gilded icons and waxen tapers
Glistened together, speaking like eyes of God.
This time, a black-robed, mightily bearded priest
Snuffed and tossed out the bank of burning candles
Like old bones from a graveyard. The blank sockets
Were filled a moment later by noisy tourists
Who clanked their shekels into a metal prayer-box.
I dropped my own coins back, deep in a pocket,
And never lit one candle against affliction
For Anne and Miles, Tess, Ginny, Israel.

Instead, retraced my steps down uneven stairs
Into a cave-shrine, wept, and pressed my hand
Against the flank of stone, the silent stone.
And felt it lean against me, as if a god
Could form itself apart from sight or speaking,
Could fill somehow the contour of human pain:
Stopped lungs, torn ligaments, abandoned children,
The ragged claw of cancer, migrant love.
*I tried so hard, six days and a long Sabbath.*
*This was the best that I could do. I'm sorry.*

# Robbie

## Accident and Essence

Whose eyes are those? Bituminous black eyes
That shine with sheer inventiveness, and love,
And when they weep, burn with a smoky flame.
Dearer than my own,
They stem from people I have never seen.

All I can say of you began the morning
You were delivered whole into my arms
And suddenly we became
Mother and child, not interlocked by blood,
Only by love's half-accidental essence.

Your cry two flights away
Startles me up the stairs and out of sleep;
I find you in the dark unerringly.
All that I don't know travels in the light
Without allusion, like a daytime ghost.

Surely the nameless parents of your birth,
Their parents' parents and collateral kin,
Must often surface on your changing face.
But I can only guess them in your smile
That stirs and answers mine.

And so they gather, fleetingly refracted,
But real to both of us:
Your birth-grandmother's gesture when she shook
Her head in disbelief, and her tall husband's
Rounded cheek, his open-throated laughter.

# Adopting Robbie

## I. Before

Three days of waiting for the ultimate yes,
The rainbow uttered on a speechless sky.
Nothing distracts us from our wish for you
Suspended somewhere in your makeshift nest,
Real, inaccessible.

You must be waking on the painted sill
Of possibility, tracing the strange
Curve and stretch of sunlight on the wall,
Sensing a presence lost.
Only a small idea to us now,

You fill the thoughts of your abstracted family,
Willing to chase the stars to Bethlehem
And find you as you are:
All that we recognize and never fathom
In any child, and all that we imagine.

## II. After

Snow stormed on your birthday,
Stormed on the day we drove
Down from the snowy mountains
To bring you home.

Night after night you wakened
At midnight, three, and seven,
Not fussing, but still hungry
For milk and me.

I fed you, and then rocked you
Beside the glinting mirror,
Running water in the bathroom
To make you sleep.

Outside the snow kept falling,
And silvered in the mirror;
I rocked you back and forth
And standing, slept.

Between our sleep and waking,
To the sound of water running,
Those nights we both endured
A second labor.

Out of the separate strangeness
We drifted slowly together,
Aching down and inward
To make one rhythm.

One smell, one long caress.
A womb of whirling snow,
And you and I together,
Safely delivered.

## Robbie Discovers Rain

Barefoot, bare headed
Except for those luxuriant black curls,
Robbie stands at play in April grass.

Rain starts suddenly, lightly,
So at first he notices
Not at all. Then touches

His curls, to find them damp and dampening.
Touches the earth, discovers
Something new that changes everything.

Looks up to know the source
And sees just leaves and air,
But goes on looking up because

—Reality or dream—
It pleases him to be
Watered by warm rain.


## Robbie Discovers Puddles

Standing in his boots, in contemplation,
He watches sun spring off the patch of water,
Then leaps. Both he and I
Start at the burst and magnitude of spray,
Our sudden decoration of muddy droplets.

"Plash," he observes, correctly, and jumps again,
While overhead a bird
Sings out its two-tone as if in applause.
Acknowledging the call, he answers, "Bird."

His joy is like mid-February sun,
Snowdrops blooming early,
The irresistible, delicious cry
Plied by the bird above. I do not say,

"Stop it. You're getting dirty. What a mess."
My irritable mother-tongue is silenced
By the great flood of light,
Two words uttered truly by my child
Splashing in boots of diamond-studded mud.

# Saying Farewell by the Bridge over the Snow River

*For Li Hua*

So you must follow after your young husband
Down the Snow River, halfway to the sea.
Too soon, before my son has learned
To understand the words
"unwilling," "travel," "mountains," "far away."
He feels your absence spun into a distance
But not in language, English or Chinese.

Now he can only stand beside the window,
Throw his toys and books across the room
Raging, wondering what the mothers
Know, and why they weep their grown-up tears.
I dreamed my son and I
Were standing on a bridge holding white flowers,
And you sailed underneath, then far beyond.

We watched your sail
Disappear between the auburn mountains.
Then there was just the unrestrained white river.
We dropped the petals slowly, one by one,
Sending them after you, until my son
Began to understand, in words like pictures.
"Boats of sandalwood, petals of magnolia."

## Robbie and I Discover Painting

Our studio is a cave behind a green door
Built into a hillside riveted by stairs
Like the improbable door I entered once
To see the ochre creatures of Altamira
Still breathless after thirty thousand years,
Flanks heaving from the chase, restrained, elusive.
How that low plastic ceiling pressed them down
On every speechless tourist, every random
Curvature of rock made flesh and bone
By some archaic brush, some vanished hand.

Now Robbie stands against his easel, speechless
Before the depths of red, black's utter midnight.
He dips and stabs: the paper's whiteness fizzles.
His mark's the birth of a new star, a nova
Blindingly there on nothing's facelessness
That also blinds. His mark is not a face,
More the proposal of his lust for pigment.
I think he wants to eat those ancient colors
Warping the paper, glutting the stubby brush
Suspended in his visible bright hand.

## Tour of the Flower Depot at Sanary-sur-Mer

The gardener, who moonlights raising flowers
Or rather, who sometimes daylights gardening,
Stands by the open doors of the great warehouse
At five a.m., and motions me inside,
Away from the bloody sunrise over Toulon.

The method of display and transportation
—Monorail carriages, whose ratchety progress
Through sale and shipment unseen powers direct—
Is Dutch: Holland controls the flower market
From Patagonia to the shoals of Iceland.

Monsieur Canolle's carnations lie in dozens
Of sorted colors, stiff in cellophane,
Fit to survive a few Saharan hours.
We pass the floral merchandise exchange
Where bids by stem and packet register

On three ten-foot clock faces on the walls.
The traders bid and smoke as the sun rises.
And then he buys me coffee in the little
Flowerless, sunless cafeteria where
Smoke spirals upward as the truckers leave.

His father and grandfather raised carnations.
But more diseases strike the flowers now,
Maladies in the water, air, and soil
That must in turn be drubbed by chemicals.
Earth, he observes, is tired of yielding flowers.

# Letting the Children Fly

*For François and Françoise De Gandt*

How strange to find the two of you at home,
Keystone for the old arch rue Mirabeau,
But all of your children flown.
Albin to another neighborhood in Paris,
Olivier to Lille, Marie, the youngest,
Translated to California. I recall her
Sweet but enigmatic, behind those owlish,
Always rose-colored glasses,
Quicksilver French I barely understood,
her Greek, her politics, her Chopin,
Expeditions down the Mekong Delta.

She calls from Berkeley. The mute telephone
Switches to "conference" so her lilting voice
Fills up the room with conversation (light)
That quickens the listeners from gray to silver.
Watching you both, so utterly attentive
To that bright shape in air,
I see her westering freedom to be gone
Stands in direct proportion to how surely,
How thoroughly you wish her home again.
To love, which, being blind,
Sees irresistibly what isn't there.

# William and Mary-Frances

Putting on the Ritz

After a long, cool winter,
At last in May a suite
Of warm days wakes the sleepers.

One covered from crown to root
In thick crepe skirtlets stops
Me, back from hibernation:

Loveliest of trees,
Big as the Ritz's balletic
Vases charged with bloom.

Not bought, not concocted,
Only improbably real.
Why am I not surprised?

My hair is snowed with silver,
Evidence how little room
Fifty springs allow.

And yet midwinter someone
Burst to life inside me,
And lately started dancing.

Just so improbably
Snow hung along the branches
Changed suddenly to flowers.

## Finitude

Awake before dawn, William and I sit drowsing,
Lapsed from a dream, louring toward consciousness,
Nursing a little, musing, counting our toes.
There are always ten, no matter where we begin.
Oh, look. He suddenly points at the closed door-windows
That cast over snow, past spindly lank silhouettes
Of maple, oak, black walnut, into the dawn.

On tiptoe, weaving, he runs up close to the windows
Charmed by the panels of gold set high among mullions
Of boles, the roses fastened in tracery branches.
Yet how the fastening ravels: our matins are sung,
The windows beyond the windows wither away,
And then he returns to my arms asking his questions
In an ancient, unknown tongue. And all of my answers,
Equally enigmatic, are kisses in shadow.

# Pirates of the Caribbean

*Disneyland*

*For Mary-Frances*

What begins as a slow drift into half-light
Suddenly accelerates: a plunge into darkness
Accompanied by rending voice-over screams
And then a world of cannon fire and carnage:
Bodies float up around us, dry land ignites.

All fake, but who's to tell you that, my smallest
Easily startled baby? In my arms
At first you wince and shiver, then go rigid—
I'd save you, but we're prisoners of a moment
Explosively contrived for older children.

So, utterly unequal to the hoopla
And razzle all around us, you give up
Turning to nurse. The pow of invented chaos
Withdraws behind the stillness of my body
That bends and opens just the same as always.

My body is your means of reckoning:
Three stars above, the Gulf Stream warm below,
My arms the coast your little craft stays close to.
Later, my love, when you set out alone
On deeper, colder waters, take my soul.

Let all the things we used to say return
Like angles among lighthouses and planets
For you to make your own triangulations,
And all we left unspoken, warmer currents
Threading the chilly maze of kelp and coral.

Material or not, my body's yearning
For the grown child it nourished once will stay:
Archipelagos scattered toward the horizon,
Involuntary tremors on the sail,
The great world rounded and a long way home.

# How Things Change

*For Helenita Izquierdo Murphy*

Holding a box of Kleenex and a grudge, I shepherd
Four complaining children across the sports-park
Groomed by unseen, incompetent civil servants.
An hour into this exercise, after I've tried
Vainly to point out impatiens, verdant mountains,
Red-orange trumpets riffing from moody hedges,
Ben and Robbie are coming to blows in the orchard,
William is losing himself in the wind-winnowed grass
Where I am sure there are snakes, and Mary-Frances
Sits on the pavement wailing, "I want to go home."
The thick air seems to be clogged with raucous goblins.

Suddenly, who should appear (we'd given up hope)
But Helenita and entourage, carrying supper.
We all troupe back to the soccer field, where the concrete
Bleachers are laid with an improvised, three-tier banquet.
But who were the goblins? Explosive, deafening, barbed,
Loading the branches of tree after tree after tree.
A cousin looks up at the leaves and shrugs. "Green parrots."
The children are running like planets in peaceful circles
Trailed by the puppy brought in to vacuum the crumbs,
And clouds part over the hills, so the lavish sunset
Can cover the earth and its offspring in azure petals.

# Fixtures of Smoke

*For Helena Izquierdo*

The parrot on the patio, magnificent, encaged,
Never stops mimicking their various voices:
Every soul in the family, grandparents, cousins,
Uncles who come in weekly from the country.
He bounces his inevitable, unseen likenesses
Off the whitewashed, bougainvillea-festooned
Wall: all day they're motives in his mad études.

Counterpoint now as Helenita's wedding dawns.
The parrot has always recorded her plaint to Helena:
"*Mamí, dónde está....*" The true voice circles the false one,
Wreathing the leaves of the lemon tree, fixtures of smoke.
Next week, Helena will wake at the edge of the patio,
Hearing her daughter's question again, as a dream-hand
Brushes a wisp of hair past a pearl-studded ear.

"*Dónde está....*" The voice-ghost triggers a sudden tear,
Then deeper grief: by the end of the rainy season,
Their foolish goblin trussed in his rose and emerald
Opera cape of feathers, gorgeous and faithless,
Feeding upside down on his meals of visceral
Watermelon, cracked seeds, detritus of lemons,
Their parrot will have forgotten that lovely voice.

# England

## After the Revolution

*For Doreen Davie*

Any American's likely to entertain
Mixed feelings for British monarchy. So I,
Transported for a season to British soil,
Have more than once been spotted at Sainsbury market
With other middle-aged ladies, shedding tears
But surreptitious, brief, for swanlike Diana,
And wondering why on earth. Perhaps the children?
Since most of us tread the swamps of maternal passion.

Yet one day squiring my black-eyed second son
To a birthday party flung by a little duchess,
I found myself escorted out of the heated
Interior lined with sixteenth century portraits,
Dotted by lamps and comfy brocaded sofas.
The garden roiled with nannies, mums, and hedges
As the maid explained she couldn't offer us tea,
Not even in the kitchen. We swept away.

"But why on earth," my friend asks as we stride
Past gilded posts of Buckingham, where the guards
Are not, this winter day, disposed to change,
"Did you decide to send the boys to Vaulted
Hall? The council schools are free, and good
Or used to be, in my day." I can't answer,
Reviewing the titled ladies, all unconscious,
Who caused my tears, saltwater stained with tea.

## Trying to Describe the Reals in Cambridge

> *"For there are two labyrinths of the human mind, one concerning the composition of the continuum, and the other concerning the nature of freedom, and they arise from the same source: infinity."*
> —G.W. Leibniz, "On Freedom"

Draw the curtains! The curtains are always closed
On roses, rugby field, light variable
But waning along these tiered northern skies
Where ten o'clock's the apogee of day,
A full moon pewtering the cliffs of sunset.
I write in the wizened glow of my computer.

I write, the Reals are really not like numbers
That we are used to count with, to begin
And go up stepwise. They are number flooded
By continuity, the line upbraided
By differential strands to labyrinth.
They are the shape and cardinal of freedom.

Abysses along abysses along abysses,
Yet perfectly defined. As if we charted
A finest-grained Grand Canyon with passing walls
Through which a sourceless unplumbed river ran,
Like moon-plate cumulant in tiers above
The river of waning sunlight. Draw the curtains!

# The Freestone Wall and the Walled Garden

*Four Variations on a Pedagogical Lecture by Jamie Redfield,
transcribed and edited by Diane Enerson*

## I. Discussion

It's a little like building a freestone wall.

Once, when I was walking in Tuscany
I met an old man building such a wall,
Who told me it was proof of God's good will,
Of providence. "I go on laying stones, until
I get a very odd-shaped empty place.
Then I reach around and lay my hand
on a rock that fits, exactly. Every time."

A good discussion class is just like that,
not every time, not always with a glass
of Chianti waiting at home to celebrate
the work of fortune.

## II. Lecture

It leaves students a certain important freedom

To pay attention or let the mind be fanned
Or ruffled by spring weather with its burden
Of bees and flowers, or both.
Who knows how many good ideas we happen
Upon though sideways windows, association
Free in the rag-and-bone shop of the heart?
Lecturing has the grace to leave us alone.

When I was at Oxford, where nobody ever discussed,
The lecture was like that: you could go sit at the back,
Take notes or write letters—the lecturers didn't care.
They left their students alone on the common assumption
That anyway all real work gets done on vacation.

## III. Discussion

Socratic discussion is very hard to do.

The only person I knew who could really use it
Was the late Joe Schwab: he made you feel he opened
Your head and drove you to think.
Before his psychoanalysis, he always
Reduced one stricken student a day to tears.
After, he only made them feel like crying.
He was absolutely ferocious: like Socrates
He always drew a crowd,
Sent you away discouraged and fascinated.

This method, of all styles,
Is most authoritative and invasive.
Employ it only with a delicate hand.

## IV. Lecture

We have a rooted objection to hierarchy

Since our post-classical civilization holds
(This is a great discovery)
Each soul is valuable and has a voice
And thus deserves a hearing. So we suppose,
Too quickly, education by discussion
Is preferable to lecture. Yet discussion

Engineers agreement through consensus.
Building a freestone wall
You cut the edges off. It's liberty,
But only within the limits of local norms.

So be a little careful. Letting be
Is often just as important as direction.
So the ecstatic interplay of blossom
And bumble bee outside a lecture hall's
Half-open window in the month of April
Is also what the lecture lets us hear.


## What Rembrandt Saw

*Portrait of Hendrickje Stoffels in the National Gallery, London*

The light tug of a pearl drop on her earlobe,
Tick of its pendulum against her throat
Measuring time's passage, or its sheer
Arrest. Here. Again, here.

The weight of two gold necklaces her breast
Warms slightly, drape incurved along a swell,
A lapse, a swell. So might he ride,
Sails furled, one summer evening on the river.

How fur on flesh is smooth and irritant.
How folds conceal by ivory impasto,
Display by contour's tributary shadow,
Rill of the dark surround.

One hand expressive, one hand self-enclosed.
Lips he has never kissed.
And that inquiring gaze: unasked, unanswered
Questions so apparent in the eye.

So shadowy. A pearl
Hangs spinning in the balance, like a world.

# Willows

*For my husband, Robert Edwards*

Along the river by the English gardens,
The dark, striated bark of willow trees
Spirals their twisted branches, doubled boles,
Till they appear like flows of lava, dense
Against the cool green downfall of their leaves.
Suspended torsion upward, animated
Leaf-flight by the thousands, strive together:
Light settles with the angel of gravity.

Our words are foliage and our solid bodies
The root of all we utter, twining upward
Through topic after topic. Round our stubborn
Union, words assume a cloudy pattern,
Thinned or excited by the breeze of passion,
Restored again in passion's settlement.


# A Bouquet for Buffalo

The loosestrife bloomed a month ago
Before we left, and still
In roadside rift and flanking swamp,
It heralds our return.

Now goldenrod is coming on,
Reminding us to mourn
Our summer and its passages
To Paris and the south.

The evening hours get small, and then
Grow larger, like the stars.
We're sorry to give August up,
Not sorry to come home,

To birch and silver maple trees
With asters at the root,
And chestnuts by the house with flat,
Half-dealt fistfuls of leaves.

Not sorry to reclaim the gray
Niagara, running north
And backward, till like destiny
It pours across the falls,

To shoals of Queen Anne's lace, a bed
Embroidered night and day
With dreams and their bright negative,
Sun-spotted reverie.

The print of violet's hooded flower
Against your cheek, and curled
In patterns on the pillowcase,
Your light, unruly hair.

And at your shadowed temple, curve
Of listening ear, that holds
To all its promises, the birds'
Low prolegomenon.

# Coming Home from England

*For my uncle, Miles Kirkpatrick, in memoriam*

Not even the most ingenious, exoteric
Gardeners in Cambridge have ever devised
Methods to keep azaleas.
Plotted across the Botanical Gardens, they fail
While everything else grows rampant:

Galaxies of narcissus and daffodil,
Chestnuts loaded with coral or ivory candles,
Lilacs. Extravagant, and yet rather pale
As if their color were leached by the constant rain,
Submerged in the flux of leaves.

But effortlessly in April
Azaleas flock the suburbs of Philadelphia
With scarlet, purple, magenta, tangerine;
Even their tailored whites are crisp and lucid.
So that's what I expected, coming home

A few days late, just after the funeral.
Instead, you're gone and the long blaze is over:
A few stray, ashy petals
Lift on the garden path when the wind spirals,
And vanish against the unmown summer grass.

# More Philosophy

## In Praise of the Humanities

*Variations on Erwin Panofsky's "The History of Art as a Humanistic Discipline."*

Nine days before his death, Immanuel Kant
Received his doctor. Ill and nearly blind,
He rose up, trembling, from his chair. The physician
Realized Kant would not sit down again
Till he himself was seated. "*Das Gefühl
Für Humanität hat mich noch nicht verlassen.*"
The visitor was moved almost to tears.

*Humanitas* has two opposed, clear meanings.
Cicero gave the classical formulation
Opposing men to beasts:
Respect for moral values, and a gracious
Blend of learning and urbanity.
Now we might call it culture.

The Middle Ages overturned this concept
By another, opposing humanity to God
And linking it with transience, frailty:
*Humanitas caduca.*

The Renaissance notion, our inheritance,
Is thoroughly ambivalent, combining
The dignity of man (freedom and reason),
And limits (error, sin, mortality).

This marriage yields the cardinal modern virtues:
Responsibility and tolerance.
The humanist, then, rejects authority,
But he respects tradition.

What use are the humanities as such?
Admittedly, they are not practical
And focus upon the past.
Why should we bother to think about the past?
The answer to both questions is just the same:
Because the real concerns us.

The life of contemplation is no less real
Than the active life, nor is what it bestows
On reality less central. As for the past,
It's no more puzzling than the elusive now.
Grasping reality
Requires a fair detachment from the present.

The sciences arrest what otherwise
Would slip away, but the humanities
Enliven what would otherwise be dead.
A subtle difference exists in Latin
Between *scientia* and *eruditio*.
*Scientia*'s possession, mastery.
*Eruditio*'s a process, more like wisdom.

History, Ficino wrote, is needed
Not just to make our lives agreeable,
But to extend their moral significance;
To make what's absent present, rejuvenate
Old things, bestow experience on the young.

Indeed, it makes of every man a Noah.
We live as many centuries as span
Our knowledge of history:
A rainbow fleeting in itself, that stays
Across the lucid gray of consciousness.


## Brancusi's Fish as a Figure of Thought

He spent so many hours just polishing
Its surfaces: two flanks
Of mirror vastly dimmed
By Parian refusal: the clenched fist,
Averted glance of marble.

But smoothing made it more percipient:
The studio walls, each form
(All twelve of them) that neighbored
Fleetingly gathered round into a space
Unlimited but finite.

Heavy, two-sided, hydroleptic, oval:
So clearly what it is
(So clarified in shape)
And yet in situ vague:
Arched and penetrated by reflection.

Just so a trout in sunlit
Riverrun replays
The place it swims through on its rainbow scales:
Continuous the way it furls and wears
The covenant of world.

# Rationalism

## I. *Cogito, Sum*

For the sake of faith,
Doubting, I held the book
And did not read.
My hand, wax-white
Against the white page,
Less real than soul,
Masked mere opinion.

O my hand, I thought,
Pitying hand and book,
You have not yet lost
Honey's strong savor,
Flower's opiate.
Nor I my heart's
Desire, dazzled sense.

## II. *Semper in abysso rerum superesse partes sopitas*

That spring I began reading Leibniz for the first time,
And failed completely to understand him.
I sat for hours far inland, under an open window,
My *Essays* crossed by the shadow of a pear tree
That bloomed, it seemed, forever just beyond me.

I was poor, illiterate, bereft, and stupid,
Unable to register love except as sex,
The white arms of the pear tree. Still some days
I longed for a dark-eyed Mediterranean, safely
Forbidden, dangerous as thought, and far, far away.

## Café on the rue Gay-Lussac

*Paris, France*

*For Martine de Gaudemar and Claude Imbert*

Exhausted, footsore, sweetening my coffee
Only with sugar, suddenly I see
That memory has lost its long allure.
I used to spend whole days remembering,
Expecting backward, painting my shabby hopes
With lipstick and mascara, trompe-l'œil glamor.

Oh Paris. Now it's only another city
Where restaurants are dear, the gutters full
Of rain and smithereens, the clerks deployed
On every front to say, *"Ah non, Madame,
C'est impossible. Vraiment, je regrette."*
Where Notre Dame is blanked by scaffolding.

All those imaginary dimensions heaped
Above my little life, like extra storeys
Hidden behind the gray-blue Mansart roofs,
Clouds crowning Sacré-Cœur, sheaves over rings,
Cotangent spaces kissing their manifold:
How finally they collapse. Goodbye, goodbye.

How finally future overshadows past
At half a hundred. What was she expecting,
That girl I was? Oh honestly, I forget.
Memory scatters in the sky like sparrows,
Or sinks like rain in gutters, where the drowned
Underground river-falls of Paris vanish.

# Days of 1984

*Woodside, California*

Time pools in the hollows, rivers of poppies
Cascade down the beds of vanished streams,
Brassy along the burnished upland pastures
Now watered only by Pacific brumes.

Can spirit burn? So I consume my hours
Stopped on this hillside, where the solar wind
Accelerates the green of Spanish grasses,
Glume, bract, and spikelet, into mottled gold.

Fountain of silence, pillar of solitude.
Impossible to say who wept for whom,
Whose fault it was, as round a pensive redwood
Foliage and shadow braid a single gloam.

Twilight fog assails the hill like tides
The moon pulls back each morning. As your voice
Rises against the steep of dreams, then fades
Down the dry channels of forgetfulness.


# Weathering

Perched in the abbey-crypt of Saint Bénigne,
The little, rotund, limestone owl is melting;
Where once medieval definition reigned,
Now just the soft crosshatch of weathering.

I have forgotten everything I studied
Wandering through here thirty years ago.
A city can't be garnered in a guide,
Nor love, it seems, in memory, although

The slant of winter sunlight on the porch
Reminds me how another accent falls.
Waiting to catch a vague electric charge,
Words are like molecules with empty shells.

Word captures word: *subjectum praedicatum*.
Despite the cinch, our lives were never one
Except in drifts indefinite as snow,
Except in lines impermanent as stone.


# Rivers

*Variations on Luna B. Leopold's "Rivers,"*
American Scientist 50, *1962, pp. 511-37*

Rain, sleet, snow, and hail's grand excess
Over evaporation and the fine,
Dense, constant transpiration of all flora,
Provides the flow of rivers.
Earth is watered by the inequation:
Congo, Mississippi, Amazon,
Yangtze, Nile, Parana,
Ob, Amur, Yanisei, and Lena.

Volumes could be written on the way
Renowned and cryptic rivers flow:
Their seasonal regimen,
Occurrence and diastole of flood waves,

Chemistry of river water, form of
River systems: snake and tree. And yet,
A poem needs restraint.
*Take up the means at hand with a good will.*

A river's organized in delicate balance,
Self-formed, self-maintained, between
Forces of erosion and resistance.
Curving the groove it runs along, it fashions
Depth, and areal figure,
Longitudinal profile, and cross-section.
Equations show its equilibrium
Studded with liquid, looped parameters:

Sheer (internal force tangential to
Ideal cross sections); bedload (particles
From bed and bank transported by the river);
Dissolved load (bedload made invisible).
Headwater pours across boulders and cobbles;
Downstream material is
Smoother, silt or silky clay. But scour
And fill tend on the average to balance.

A river overflows its banks in flood.
Everywhere, in rivers of all sizes,
Bankfull stages happen once a year, or
Once in two. The floodplain
Has to drown biennially, and proves
Inherent to a river.
*What are we? Indeed, what are we not?*
*Ephemeral, the light dream of a shadow.*

Despite the broad necessity of floods,
Most fluvial work on landscape forms

Stems from intermediate events:
A modest count of days of
Intermediate flow or scour. Like love;
Like ordinary science with its careful,
Incomplete descriptions. *Let us be
Small in small things, great in greater things.*

Nearly every natural channel snakes.
(Indeed, a river's rarely a straight line
Longer than ten channel widths.)
Meandering or merely sinuous,
Curves a channel carves
Remain in constant ratio to its girth:
Small channels wind in smaller, great in greater
Curves. The noblest element is water.

Sinuosity's root cause is just
How water flows: hydro-
Dynamics. Independent of its load,
Any river slowly, surely migrates
Laterally across the valley floor.
The laws of water run
Beyond the little rules that order stone,
Farmers, or the fan of delta soil.

*Seek not, my soul, the life of the immortals.*
Even among the very smallest rills and
Broadest river basins,
Logarithmic proportions hold
Between stream order and the length of streams
Of given lesser order, and between
Stream order and the multitude of streamlets.
Rivers most resemble trees,

Not just as schema, but as organism:
Parts arranged dynamically in
Causal, mutual self-regulation.
Given possible discharge and prevailing
Channel characters, a graded stream
Is delicately adjusted to provide
The one precise velocity required for
Transport of the load.

Thus rivers freely flow
According to the principle of least work,
That, like the *Odes* of Pindar, gently governs
Spirit wound in matter's labyrinth.
So the river-snake's a tree,
Tree a form of systematic thought,
Thought, like us, an asymmetrical,
Branched mirror of God.

## The Historian's Pursuit

*For Christine Leigh Heyrman*

A nation founded on oblivion,
Relentlessly forgetful, we send you down
Instead of us to occupy the past
In rental cars, motel rooms, August heat
Quilting the Piedmont like an ocean *redux*.

Dust-riddled boxes under the county courthouse,
And figures—faded brown ink scrawled or printed—
Deliver up small lives in all their scant
Nobility: how one outwitted death
By fire, or fed unmarriageable daughters,
Or shouted God awake in the big tents
Like ersatz battlefields
For disappointed antebellum youth.

It seems that men must have their bloody conflicts
Even when all hostilities have ceased,
Even when blood's transmuted back to grape juice
(Baptist wine) and carnage to loaves of bread.

Day after day, you leaf through
Cartons of mixed-up, yellowed information
Letters, deeds, tax records, census findings
Driven by our amnesia, your conviction
That taken line by line they must mean *something*.
One box, one courthouse, one hypothesis
Leads you a little farther down the silent
Back roads crossing Carolina pine woods
Where summer long since pressed the redbuds dry.

# Signing the Darkness

*Upon an e-mail from Patricia Book*

We spent the evening kayaking, or dreaming
Along a channel lined with mangrove trees
Whose tannin dyes the blood-warm water red.
Imported and free iguanas overhead
Slept sticking to the trees, and here and there
A termite nest degraded nutrients.
Our channel metamorphosed to a brackish
Inland lagoon where all at once the paddles
Thrillingly stirred up luminescent algae.
Adrift, we watched the other kayaks loom
Signing the darkness with their phosphor plumes,
One wake by each of them.

We settled over the heart of the lagoon,
Slid off our kayaks into the black water,
And saw each other outlined like submerged
But glowing angels, algae's benediction.
Then reembodied on a fishing boat
To toast our progress with a short Merlot,
Crunchy asparagus sandwiches, barbecued hot
Chicken in guava sauce, a Russian chorus.
Then fled in the kayaks, backward with the current
Too fast. We never want such dreams to end,
Though since they haunt the memory ever after,
We never wake from them.

## Ithaka II

Penelope held off her ravenous suitors
By promising, tomorrow and tomorrow,
She'd finish lost Ulysses' winding sheet.
The Greek text says that she composed in light,

And analyzed in darkness. Woven figures
Unraveled are not quite analysis,
Rather a woman trying to understand
The altitude and basis of her island.

All day Penelope addressed the warp,
Her shuttle a small craft with two directions.
All night her solitude relit the torch.
To analyze is to set life in question,

Despite the crush of suitors at the door,
The cold synthetic wave raking the shore.

## Watering

Trying to revive the variegated
Flowers I planted fast and then abandoned
For last month's trip, I stand
Patient, absorbed, hot.
Midsummer's wilting downdraft serpents up.

Banded by that warm air rising and rising,
I press the stone-cold lever on the hose:
A stream of water darkens the earth, mocking,
Saving a few of my bright bedding plants.

I see, no matter where the spray's directed,
A brief, truncated spectrum,
Light cut short and plagued by interference,
But rife with all the colors nonetheless.

O divine will I cannot rise to meet,
Who span the whole sky with galactic arches,
Be patient with me here.
Forgive my false starts, limping finishes.

At least occasionally I seem to make
Fragmentary rainbows, and to set
Their pluvial effects in the right places,
Not only for the gardener's amusement,
But for the garden's sake.

*Acknowledgments*

I am grateful to the editors of the following journals where many of these poems originally appeared, sometimes in slightly different forms:

*A Year*

*Able Muse:* "Daylilies," "Days of 1983," "Silver"

*The Hudson Review:* "Ode to the Butterflies," "The Always Coming On," "Where the Wild Things Are," "In Praise of Fractals," "The Choir," "What a Poet Wants," "Technical Divination," "Justice," "On Painting," "Morning Delivery of *The Times*," "Elegy," "Two Meditations on Stone," "Mind," "The Beautiful Game," "Where I Went and Cannot Come Again," "Kisses," "The Stars of Earth," "Equal and Opposite," "Roses," "November," "Not Summer," "Spring Cleaning," "While You Lay Sleeping," "What I Forgot, What I Could Not Forget," "Abbey Road," "Elegy for the Tussey Ridge: Fracking Comes to Central Pennsylvania," "Love's Shadow"

*Sewanee Review:* "The House of Trees," "The Dream of Chaucer," "On Pilgrim Hill," "The Art of Glassblowing," "Citizens," "Letter from Châtel-Montagne," "Forsythia," "Sunset," "Leaves and Clouds"

*PN Review:* "Four from the Berggarten, Hannover," "Astronomy," "Insomnia," "The Tallinn Ferry," "European Paper," "Leaving the Garden," "Holding Pattern"

*Watershed:* "Snowdrop," "Bittersweet," "Goodbye to State College"

*The San Diego Reader:* "Counterpane," "Uncertain"

*American Scientist:* "Among Cosmologists"

*American Suzuki Journal:* "First Piano Lesson"

*The Mathematical Intelligencer:* "Elliptic Curves and Modular Forms Converge South of the Taklamakan"

*Green Mountains Review:* "Where the Wild Things Are"

*American Arts Quarterly:* "Ut musica pictura"

*Prairie Schooner:* "Primary School," "The Kitchen Window"

*Southern Review:* "Two Passages from Colette"

*Centre Daily Times:* "Twelfth Night"

*Sanctuary:* "April 7, 2011"

*Blue Lyra Review:* "Here and There"

*The River Painter*

*The Hudson Review:* "Letter from Germany," "Galerie Orphée," "In the Light of October," "97 rue Compans," "Dinner in the Courtyard," "In the Garden," "The Last of the Courtyard"

*The Kenyon Review:* "The Dissolution of the Rainbow," "Marathon"

*Cumberland Poetry Review:* "Ithaka I," "On an Album Leaf by Ma Yuan," "Birds, Trees and Lovers"

*Poetry:* "The River Painter," "Gathering of Friends, after the Fall of the Sung Dynasty"

*New England Review:* "The Return"

*The Iowa Review:* "In Medias Res"

*Harper's:* "Edgewood Park"

*The Massachusetts Review:* "Following the Dordogne"

*The St. Andrews Review:* "On the Ferry, toward Patras"

*The Black Warrior Review:* "Rodin to Rilke"

*Calyx:* "On the Loss of My Mother's Jewelry"

*South and West:* "Ruins at Jumièges"

*Connecticut Artists:* "To Cathy Iino"

*Shores and Headlands*

*The Hudson Review:* "Letters from La Plata," "The Outer Banks," "Open Secrets," "The Courtyard Revisited," "The Tempest," "The Cliffs at Praiano"

*Prairie Schooner:* "In the Abruzzi"

*Cumberland Poetry Review:* "Mediterranean," "The Gold Earrings," "Saint-Germain, Paris, France"

*Poetry:* "Siesta," "The Old Fisherman"

*Kairos:* "After Timaeus"

*The Yale Review:* "The Warning"

*Michigan Quarterly Review:* "Two Variations on a Theme"

*Pequod:* "Nietzsche in the Box of Straws"

*Boulevard:* "Another Song"

*Eden*

*The Hudson Review:* "On Spadina Avenue," "Dark Tents and Fires," "Rain or Shine," "Autumn Sonata"

*New England Review:* "Life of a Salesman"

*New Virginia Review:* "Excursion to the Third *Calanque*," "Proportions of the Heart," "The Shape of Desire"

*Partisan Review:* "Two Passages from Colette"

*Pequod:* "Pilgrims," "The Neolithic Revolution of 1956"

*Pivot:* "Waiting for News of Jackie's Firstborn"

*Poetry:* "Thirty-Six Weeks"

*Prairie Schooner:* "Sidonie"

*Raritan:* "Symmetry," "The Pot of Basil"

*Sewanee Theological Review:* "Listening"

*The Southern Review:* "Commuter Marriage"

*The Hudson Review:* "Anna," "Where the Sky Used to Be," "Tour of the Flower Depot at Sanary-sur-Mer," "Rondo, Andante," "Finitude," "The Abacus of Years," "Robbie and I Discover Painting"

*The American Scholar:* "Brancusi's Fish as a Figure of Thought"

*Connecticut Review:* "Adopting Robbie"

*Critical Quarterly* (England): "Revisiting the Church of the Holy Sepulcher"

*The Formalist:* "Willows"

*Lilt:* "Robbie Discovers Rain"

*Michigan Quarterly Review:* "Accident and Essence," "Through the Darkness Be Thou Near Me"

*New Letters:* "Watering"

*Poetry:* "The Great Blizzard," "Pirates of the Caribbean"

*Poetry Review* (London)*:* "What Rembrandt Saw"

*Prairie Schooner:* "Real Bullets," "Robbie Discovers Puddles," "Saying Farewell by the Bridge over the Snow River," "Putting on the Ritz"

*Princeton University Library Chronicle:* "A Bouquet for Buffalo"

*Rafters:* "Cogito, Sum"

A number of these poems were included in the following chapbooks, which I was happy to create along with artists Farhad Ostovani, Lucy Vines Bonnefoy, Robert Fathauer and the late Chihiro Iwasaki, along with music composed by Bruce Trinkley, Kaori Muraji, Koko Tanikawa, and Mirco De Stefani.

*Childhood* (poems, with drawings by Lucie Vines Bonnefoy). Accents Publishing, 2014. This book has raised over $2500 for UNICEF since it was launched.

*Infanzia.* An Italian translation by Sara Amadori (University of Bologna). Raffaelli Editore (Rimini), 2016.

こどもの時間 A Japanese translation by Atsuko Hayakawa (Tsuda College, Tokyo). Kurumed Shuppan, 2015.

*Enfance*. A French translation by Pascale Drouet (University of Poitiers). 2018.

*Proportions of the Heart: Poems that Play with Mathematics*. Tessellations Publishing, 2014.

*Feuilles / Leaves* (poems, with Farhad Ostovani). William Blake & Co., 2007. This chapbook includes a series of Farhad Ostovani's *Goldberg Variations*, and a suite of my poems with French translations by Alain Madeleine-Perdrillat *en face*.


Many of these poems have also been included in the following anthologies:

*Bridges 2016* and *Bridges 2013*, ed. Sarah Glaz, Tessellations Publishing; *Mortals and Immortals* (Celebration of the thirty-fifth Anniversary of the Burchfield Penney Art Center), ed. Don Metz, Blaze Vox, 2014; *Poets Translate Poets*, ed. Paula Deitz, Syracuse University Press, 2013; *Penguin's Poems for Love*, ed. Laura Barber, Penguin Books, 2009; *Strange Attractors: Poems of Love and Mathematics*, eds. JoAnne Growney and Sarah Glaz, A.K. Peters, Ltd., 2008; *The Shape of Content: Creative Writing in Mathematics and Science*, eds. M. Senechal, C. Davis, J. Zwicky, A.K. Peters, Ltd., 2008; *Conversation Pieces: Poems that Talk to Other Poems*, ed. K. Brown, Knopf, Everyman's Library, 2007; *Rhyming Poems: A Contemporary Anthology*, ed. W. Baer, University of Evansville Press, 2007; *Lineas conectadas: neuva poesía de Estados Unidos / Connecting Lines: New Poetry from the United States*, ed. A. Lindner, a bilingual two-volume anthology where poems are presented in both English and Spanish, Sarabande Books, 2006; *Norton Introduction to Literature*, ninth edition and Shorter ninth edition, eds. J.P. Hunter, K. Mays, A. Booth, Norton, 2005; *Western Wind: An Introduction to Poetry*, eds. D. Mason and J.F. Nims, McGraw-Hill, 2005; Contemporary *American Poetry*, eds. R.S. Gwynn and A. Lindner, Pearson / Longman / Penguin, 2005; *Women's Writing: Past and Present*, ed. C. Zilboorg, Cambridge Contexts in Literature, Cambridge University Press, 2004; *Words Brushed by Music: The Best Poems from the First 25 Years of the Johns Hopkins Poetry Series*, ed. J. Irwin, Johns Hopkins University Press, 2004; *Poetry in Motion from Coast to Coast: 120 Poems from the Subways and the Buses*, eds. E. Paschen and B. Fletcher, Norton, 2002; *The Norton Introduction to Literature*, eight edition, eds. J.P. Hunter, K. Mays, J. Beaty, Norton, 2002; *The Spirit of Pregnancy*, ed. B. Goldberg, Contemporary

Books, 2000; *Verse and Universe: Poems on Science and Mathematics,* ed. K. Brown, Milkweed Press, 1998; *Rebel Angels: 25 Poets of the New Formalism,* eds. M. Jarman and D. Mason, Story Line Press, 1996; *Formal Introductions: An Investigative Anthology,* ed. D. Gioia, Aralia Press, 1994; *An Introduction to Poetry* (eight, ninth, tenth edition) and *Literature: An Introduction to Fiction, Poetry, and Drama,* eds. X.J. Kennedy and D. Gioia, HarperCollins Publishers, 1993/94 – 2002; *A Formal Feeling Comes: Poems in Conspicuous Form by Contemporary Women,* ed. A. Finch, Story Line Press, 1993/4; *Articulations: The Body and Illness in Poetry,* ed. J. Mukand, Iowa City: University of Iowa Press, 1994; *The Virago Book of Birth Poems,* ed. C. Otten, Virago Press, 1993; *Parallels: Artists/Poets,* New York: Midmarch Arts Press, 1993; *Love Poems by Women,* ed. W. Mulford, Ballantine Books, 1990; *Gathered Waters,* ed. Cort Conley, Backeddy Books, 1985.

Emily Grosholz was born in the suburbs of Philadelphia, and attended the University of Chicago and Yale University. Since 1979 she has taught at the Pennsylvania State University, where she is now Edwin Erle Sparks Professor of Philosophy, African American Studies, and English. Her first book of poetry, *The River Painter,* appeared in 1984; her most recent book, *Childhood,* has been translated into Japanese, Italian and French, and has raised $2500 for UNICEF. Her  translation from the French of Yves Bonnefoy's *Beginning and End of the Snow* was published in 2012. She has lived in France, Germany, and the UK, and traveled to Japan, Russia, Costa Rica, and around the Mediterranean and the Baltic. Since 1984, she has been an advisory editor for *The Hudson Review*. She and her husband, Robert Edwards, raised four children in State College, Pennsylvania, on the flanks of the Tussey Ridge, countryside that they and their neighbors, with the ClearWater Conservancy, are working to protect and preserve. She teaches at the West Chester Poetry Conference and at Writing the Rockies in the summer. Her book, *Great Circles: The Transits of Mathematics and Poetry,* will be published in 2018 by Springer.

*The Stars of Earth: New and Selected Poems* (Word Galaxy Press, 2017) is her eighth book of poetry.

ALSO FROM WORD GALAXY PRESS

Margaret Rockwell Finch, *Crone's Wines: Late Poems*

A.G. Harmon, *Some Bore Gifts – Stories*

Elizabyth A. Hiscox, *Reassurance in Negative Space – Poems*

www.wordgalaxy.com

www.ingramcontent.com/pod-product-compliance
Lightning Source LLC
Chambersburg PA
CBHW020221170426
43201CB00007B/279